THE GOLF PRĬMER

A MANUAL FOR

THE ADULT BEGINNER

AND

HIGH HANDICAP PLAYER

W. R. Miller
Professor and Dean
The University of Missouri
Columbia, MO

illustrated by
Terry L. Martin
William Woods College
Fulton, MO

graphic layout by
Amy E. Hess
Columbia, MO

PineCrest Publications, P. O. Box 71, Sautee-Nacoochee, GA 30571

PineCrest Publications

Copyright 1991
by
W. R. Miller
Professor and Dean
University of Missouri
Columbia, Missouri

Printed in the United States of America
Library of Congress Cataloging in Publication Data
91-90077
The Golf Primer/ W. R. Miller
p. 136   cm. 21.25 x 27.5
ISBN 0-9628887-0-2

Suggested List Price $29.95

A MESSAGE TO

INSTRUCTORS AND STUDENTS

The adult learner needs knowledge and understanding of the various physical, mental and emotional aspects of the game of golf. Knowledge and understanding provide a foundation upon which the various elements of the game can be built. *The Golf Primer* is the student's textbook. It is a daily reference to help reinforce and compliment instruction. Before and after each practice session or lesson, *The Golf Primer* is the student's guide to understanding, review, and reflection.

Adult students need a total development program that includes (1) reading and study, (2) small group and individual instruction by a qualified professional over a sustained period of time, followed by (3) an intensive period of instruction such as provided by a golf school or academy.

An effective developmental program requires a substantial commitment of time and monetary resources to get a good start on the road to improvement, consistency and enjoyment. The bottom line for most adults who play golf should be enjoyment. It is a leisure time activity that has the potential for enhancing our lives. Golf is the type of game that is never mastered. It can be played on various levels depending on the player's expectations and competence.

Your commitment of time and resources to a total development program is the surest route to enjoyment of the game. *The Golf Primer* is a part of your development program. Study it thoroughly as you improve and enjoy the challenging game of golf.

Best Wishes,

W. R. Miller

i

ACKNOWLEDGEMENTS

When one engages in a project of this magnitude, the time and talent of many individuals are involved. The author acknowledges with special appreciation the contributions of PGA professionals, Andy Prosowski, Golf Schools of Scottsdale, Arizona; Fred Griffin, The Grand Cypress Academy of Golf at Grand Cypress Resort in Orlando, Florida; Greg Ortman, The Woodlands Golf Academy at Nemocolin Woodlands Resort in Farmington, Pennsylvania; and Ann Casey Johnstone, former golf coach at Stephens College, LPGA master teacher and golf clinician who provided both encouragement and a critical review of the manuscript. In addition, both formal and informal input was received from local PGA professionals, Brad Hulett of the Columbia Country Club, Richard Poe, Country Club of Missouri and men's golf coach and Mary McNabb Scott, women's golf coach at the University of Missouri.

Communicating the technical aspects of the static and dynamic parts of the golf swing cannot be accomplished with words alone. The illustrations provided by Terry Martin are invaluable in communicating the essential body positions and movements for an effective golf swing. Appreciation is also expressed to many talented professionals whose writings have influenced the author even though they were unaware of their influence, namely, Dr. Richard Coop, Dr. Gary Wiren, Michael Hebron, Ken Venturi, Dr. DeDe Owens, Dave Pelz, Tom Watson, Tom Kite, Dr. Jim Suttie, John Redman, Paul Runyan, Gary Player, and many others. Special thanks to the staff of PineCrest Publications, especially Dr. M.F. Kraska whose editorial and promotional talents made this publication possible.

The cooperation of the directors of selected golf schools and academies is acknowledged with appreciation. The opportunity to attend several of these programs enabled the author to secure photographs and descriptions for inclusion in this publication.

ABOUT THE AUTHOR

Dr. W. R. Miller is a native of Missouri and a graduate of the University of Missouri-Columbia where he received his baccalaureate, masters, and doctoral degrees.

After teaching in the Hazelwood School District in suburban St. Louis and the University Laboratory School in Columbia, Missouri, Dr. Miller taught at Purdue University in West Lafayette, Indiana. In 1963, Dr. Miller returned to the University of Missouri-Columbia where he moved through the ranks from Assistant to Full Professor in the College of Education. Through the years he served as a Department Chair, as Associate Dean, and as Dean of the College of Education.

Dr. Miller authored or co-authored three professional books, edited an industrial arts series, and contributed more than 40 articles in professional journals, monographs, and yearbook chapters. The focus of Dr. Miller's research, teaching, and scholarship has been on the professional development of the technical specialist as a teacher. His book, *Instructors and Their Jobs*, is considered to be a classic in the field of technical teacher education.

The author was involved in team sports until age 30, when he was introduced to golf by a well-intentioned friend. Unfortunately, it was not until a decade later, with 18-hole scores between 95 and 100, that he took his first formal golf lesson. For the next ten years, Dr. Miller took a couple of lessons each year, which improved his game to the point that most 18-hole scores were in the high 80's. During the third ten year period, the author gained *knowledge* and *understanding* of the mechanics of the four basic strokes of golf that should have formed the foundation for the first ten years. This knowledge and understanding led to a level of competence and consistency whereby competitive 18-hole scores were generally between 75 and 80. If the knowledge and understanding, presented in *The Golf Primer*, could have been acquired earlier, the rocky road would have been much smoother and the progress much faster. (Appendix D)

As a result of (1) first-hand experience, (2) countless hours of study, (3) interaction with some of the country's best professional golf instructors, and (4) the perspective of a professional educator, Dr. Miller has provided the adult beginner and high handicap player with a proven method to improvement, consistency and satisfaction in the game of golf.

PREFACE

The purpose of this instruction manual is to provide adult beginners or high handicap players with the fundamentals necessary to develop their ability to stroke the golf ball. In a nutshell, this manual will provide you with the basic principles involved in making the four strokes (putting, chipping, pitching, and full swing) inherent in the game of golf. This manual is designed for the mature adult who is interested and willing to make an investment of time and resources. An investment of time is necessary to develop the psychomotor skills necessary to stroke the golf ball effectively. Consistency, power, and accuracy are relative terms and individuals differ in their abilities to achieve in these three areas. However, when you acquire the fundamental techniques described and illustrated in this manual, you will be limited only by your body type, strength, flexibility, coordination, and other personal factors, e.g., your personal commitment to practice, mental toughness, and concentration. Resources must be invested for equipment and professional instruction.

The fundamentals described and illustrated in this manual are those that I wish I had known and understood as a beginner. My road from 120 strokes for 18 holes to less than 80 strokes has indeed been rocky. I could have had much greater success much sooner if I had "been on the right track." I have used my skills and experience as a professional educator to analyze, describe, illustrate and otherwise communicate the essential positions and movements necessary to the development of psychomotor skills related to the four strokes of the game of golf.

Golf is a game for a lifetime. If you "get on the right track" by building a foundation of correct techniques and developing a positive mental outlook, you can have many years of enjoyment and satisfaction.

CONTENTS

INTRODUCTION

Making an effective and efficient stroke with a golf club is both a mental and a physical action. You must have knowledge of certain positions and motions to be made by the body. Signals must be sent to the muscles in order to change thoughts into action. The term neuromuscular is often used to describe this complex process by which thoughts are transformed into physical action. In the process of developing psychomotor skills, it is important to (1) understand the movements to be made, (2) convert knowledge and understanding of movement into a mental picture, (3) make the movements slowly and correctly, (4) gradually increase the speed of the movements and (5) repeat the correct movements until they become a thoroughly established habit. The process of developing a new skill is much simpler than unlearning a set of neuromuscular movements and replacing them with a set of similar, yet different, neuromuscular movements. Even if you have never swung a golf club before, you may have some neuromuscular "reinforcement" as well as "interference" from a previous activity such as swinging a baseball bat. I can assure you as one who played competitive league baseball and softball until the age of 30, there is both positive and negative transfer from the neuromuscular activity of swinging a bat to the swinging of a golf club. In fact, I consider the movement of the two activities to have as many differences as similarities. The observation that good baseball players or good tennis players often develop into good golfers can be attributed more to well developed body mechanics, coordination and strength than to any similarity of the psychomotor skills involved.

Even though the body movements that are necessary to execute the golf swing, have been analyzed in detail, it is not necessary for a beginning golfer to understand all of the intricacies involved. This manual is written in a deliberate attempt to provide you with only the movements and descriptions that are judged essential to successful execution. From the standpoint of effective learning and skill development, you need to have a total concept of both the static (still) and dynamic (moving) parts of the swing. Further, it is important that you understand the relationship that the different segments or parts of the swing have to each other. This knowledge and understanding will enable your brain to do a better job of sending signals to your muscles as the various movements are made.

Please know that I am aware that individuals have taken up the game of golf with little or no knowledge of the techniques involved in executing the golf swing. Some of them have done a reasonably good job of moving the ball from tee to green. The more successful of those persons who "pick up" the game through observation and trial and error learning typically have well developed physical coordination, body mechanics, and hand-eye coordination. These individuals soon reach a plateau in their performance level and cannot maximize their special talents because of a lack of knowledge and understanding of swing techniques. The most unfortunate part of this scenario is that this moderately successful individual develops some incorrect body movements that become a neuromuscular habit with a substantial amount of "muscle memory." (A misnomer, since a muscle does not have a memory.) For an

1

individual to get off a "performance plateau" and begin to improve, he or she will need to "unlearn" certain movements and acquire some similar although different movements. This process is difficult and almost certainly results in a lower level of performance until the newer and more correct movements have become habits. Some individuals are unwilling to accept this apparent "backward step" or the investment in time, frustration and ego deflation that is often necessary to get off a comfortable road that leads nowhere to a road that offers a better opportunity for improvement and consistency.

This instructional manual is not designed for individuals who have already developed the fundamentals of the four basic strokes. The manual was not written by a successful professional golfer or a former professional golfer. The author is first and foremost a teacher who has taught adults for more than thirty-five years. The author, nearly thirty years ago, at age 30 decided to take up golf. This manual is the result of more than twenty-five years of taking lessons, attending special instructional schools, reading, analyzing and working with adults learning to stroke the golf ball. You must be reminded that this Primer does not attempt to cover all of the subtle nuances that every "expert" has found to be helpful to certain individuals with certain physical and/or psychological characteristics.

This manual is for the adult beginner and high handicap player and should be regarded as your *PRIMER*. It provides a foundation and a beginning point. As you grow and develop in your understanding and skill level you will need specialized attention that only a qualified professional instructor can provide. I can assure you that learning the basic strokes of golf and applying them to the game of golf is a developmental process that takes an investment of your resources (time and money). There is no quick fix. There is no "one magic move" or "one magic club" that brings instant success. The author recognizes the limitations of this instruction manual. It will not serve all of your developing needs as a golfer. As you increase in your skill and understanding, you will have unique needs and interest that can be best met through direct instruction by a qualified golf instructor, attending golf instructional schools and academies, viewing golf instructional videos and reading golf instructional books and magazines. Even as you become an accomplished player, you will profit by returning to your *PRIMER* and concentrating on stroke fundamentals. As you grow in your knowledge and understanding of the intricacies of the game, regardless of your skill level, you will become, as Arnold Palmer says, "A golfer and not just someone who plays golf."

> *"Golf is a test, not so much of the muscle, or even of the brain and nerves of a man as it is a test of his inmost veriest self; of his soul and spirit; of his whole character and disposition; of his temperament; of his habit of mind, of the entire content of his mental and moral nature as handed down to him by unnumbered multitudes of ancestors."*
> *Arnold Haultain*

As inscribed in the PGA World Golf Hall of Fame, Pinehurst, NC

CHAPTER 1

GOLF: THE GAME FOR A LIFETIME

This manual, as indicated in the Preface, is not designed to tell you "all you ever wanted to know about the game of golf." It is, rather, a PRIMER limited to the fundamentals of the four basic strokes necessary to play the game with even a minimum degree of success and personal satisfaction. Nevertheless, the teacher in me feels compelled to describe the fundamental rules of the game, the etiquette of the game, and to share a bit of the philosophy of life that seems to be symbolized in the game. We will leave it to others to chronicle the game's illustrious history, to present a more extensive set of rules and to describe the amateur and professional organizational activities devoted to the maintenance of standards and traditions.

FUNDAMENTALS OF THE GAME

Whether the game of golf is played over a course containing nine greens (putting areas) or 18, the game involves a process of stroking the golf ball with one or more of the four basic strokes (putting, chipping, pitching and the full swing) from a beginning point, called the teeing area or tee box, to a green which contains the ultimate target, "the cup," into which a slender pole with a flag attached (the *flag stick* or *stick*) is inserted. The grassy area between the tee and the green is referred to as "fairway" and is mowed at a height of 1 1/2 - 2 inches. Other areas outside the fairway are referred to as "rough" and contain longer grass, bushes, trees, sand areas (bunkers), water and other hazard areas where the ball may be difficult to locate and even more difficult to stroke properly.

The entire area from tee to cup is referred to as a "hole." Depending on the distance from tee to green, the player chooses a club that, when swung correctly, will propel the ball as close to green and cup as possible. (See Figure 0-2 in Glossary.) The length of a standard golf "hole" is 251 to 470 yards for men and 211 to 400 for women. The standard number of strokes from tee to cup referred to as "par" is four—two strokes to the green and two putting strokes. Most holes on a golf course are standard and have a par of four. Some holes, however, are shorter (typically 100-250 yards for men and up to 210 for women) and are designated as having a par of three. On a hole designated as a par three, the expectation is that the proficient player will stroke the ball once from tee to green and use two putting strokes to get the ball into the cup. In addition to a few par threes, the course usually has several holes that are longer than the standard par four which may be from 471 to 600 yards for men and up to 575 yards for women. The standard number of strokes for holes of this length is five.

Occasionally, a course will have a par six hole of over 575 yards for women. A proficient player is expected to take three strokes to reach the green and two putting strokes to roll the ball into the cup. With an average of four strokes expected on each of 18 holes the par for the game would be 72. A nine hole game would be one-half of eighteen and par would be 36. Golf courses are constructed with this general format although the combination of holes that are par 4, 3, 5, and an occasional 6 may result in a total course par of 70, 71, 72 or on occasion 73. (See Figure 0-3 in Glossary, p. 13.)

THE SYMBOLISM: GOLF AND LIFE

In many ways golf is a silly game that for some individuals takes on proportions larger than life itself. Golf, as life, brings out the full range of human emotions; from elation to despair; from joy to sorrow; gentility to rage; integrity to fraud. In golf, as in life, self is exposed to the divine as the ultimate judge. The game pits the individual alone against the course with a set of standard tools (clubs) and a book of rules to guide him or her on the journey represented by 18 fairways and greens or nine, as the case may be. The game may have a social dimension if played and enjoyed with others, or it may provide an opportunity for reflective solitude as you may choose. As in life, the destination is known, but the route may be circuitous and strewn with many unexpected circumstances.

Even after the basic fundamentals have been learned, there are many unexpected consequences of our actions. For our mind to transmit the appropriate signals to cause our muscles to make the correct movements which will swing the club on the desired path is, indeed, a challenge. Aside from the swing, or stroke, variables there are many other variables to be considered as decisions are made. Variables such as the ground under the ball, "Does it slope? If so, in what direction? How much?" How far does the ball need to travel? Does the trajectory need to be high or low? Is the green

elevated or is it lower than the ball? Are there trees that might come into play? Is the grass long or short? Is the grass wet or dry?

One's journey through life also requires many decisions, and there are many variables to be considered. When one makes a decision or takes an action, "What is the result?" Does the ball end up behind a tree, in a ditch, in the rough, on the green, or in the cup? If it is behind a tree, in a ditch, or in the rough, it is comparable to one of life's adversities. How will you handle it? What mental, emotional and physical powers within yourself will you draw upon to deal with the situation. Human beings deal with adversity in many ways and these variations are mirrored in one's behavior on the golf course as well. As revealed by Plato, "You can discover more about a person in an hour of play than in a year of conversation."

GOLF IS A GAME

Golf is a great game if approached in proper perspective as a game. Of course you will want to do your best. However, you must be true and fair with yourself and your limitations. Each of us has a limited amount of potential for achievement because of individual differences in our human qualities or natural abilities. Even though we know our potential is limited, it should be emphasized that very few of us work to our maximum potential. Nevertheless, your potential is a variable, and it will determine the outer limits of your performance. There are many instances in which a person of average ability out performs an individual with greater natural ability. However, the fact that some individuals have greater potential than others is still a reality. Fortunately, the game of golf pits the individual against the course, and no comparisons with other individuals need to be made. Obviously, when one chooses to engage in golf competition, individual performances are compared. Competition with others, however, is not an inherent quality of the game of golf. You have a choice in this regard.

> *To play golf is to run the entire gamut of human emotions not only in a brief space of time, but likewise without measurable damage to ourselves or to others.*
>
> *The game as played on the golf course represents only a modest part of the pleasure, enjoyment and satisfaction that comes to a person because he is a golfer.*
>
> *One of the very important attractions of golf is that it provides a wide and varied assortment of topics for conversation.*
>
> *The lore of the game, the story of its development and of the stirring deeds of the great players of the past must always command the respectful attention of those who play golf at all regularly.*

Robert T. Jones Jr.
As inscribed in the PGA World Golf Hall of Fame, Pinehurst, NC

It is appropriate to acknowledge that you have physical limits and to recognize that you are limited in the amount of time you may be able to devote to practice, a very important element in psychomotor skill development. Keeping the game in its proper perspective for you involves setting reasonable goals and having reasonable expectations. As a beginner, you should avoid comparisons with others. Measure your success in terms of your personal goals, your level of improvement in the different aspects of the game, (the four basic strokes—putting, chipping, pitching and the full swing).

The game of golf uses a "handicap" system that allows players of unequal ability to have their scores adjusted for competitive purposes (See Glossary, page 10.) If your average score is approximately 120 strokes for 18 holes, you would have a handicap of between 40 and 45. On a given day, your gross score could be 115 strokes less a handicap of 43 which would result in a net 72, or par, for the course. However, do not allow yourself to use "score" as the only measure of success or satisfaction. Focus instead on the stroke fundamentals. Learn to make solid contact between club and ball with each stroke. Set practice goals, e.g., make 4 of 6 putts from 5 feet; stroke 5 of 10 chips within 3 feet of the cup from a distance of 15 yards; pitch 5 of 15 balls into a 15 foot diameter circle from 50 yards. When playing a golf hole that has a par of 4, you as a beginner, should not expect the same score as an expert player. Instead, you should adjust your expectations to 6, 7, or 8 strokes. Just as in life one must find ways to gain positive reinforcement through the process of living. We have often been admonished to "smell the roses along the way." So it is with golf. The game is played in nature's most pleasant surroundings. The sky, trees, lakes, streams, flowers, and grass form the backdrop for the game. Walking, bending, and stretching are great exercise.

In addition, the game requires concentration which can divert one's thoughts from life's adversities that create much stress. However, if not kept in proper perspective, this "silly" game can produce as much stress and tension as any adversity we encounter in our lives. Perhaps you can keep in mind Sir Winston Churchill's remark, "Golf is a curious sport whose object is to put a very small ball in a very small hole with implements ill designed for the purpose."

Take the time necessary to understand and execute the movements necessary to develop the skills inherent in the four basic strokes essential to the game of golf. This manual is designed to "put you on the right track" so that you can gain satisfaction and enjoyment from a lifetime of golf.

RULES AND ETIQUITTE GOVERNING GOLF

As previously indicated a set of rules, like those of most games, has been developed for the game of golf. As an aspiring player of the game, you should acquire a set of rules which are available in booklet form from the United States Golf Association (USGA). A condensed version is also available through most golf course professionals. Most of the rules have their antecedents in the deliberations of the Royal and Ancient Golf Club of St. Andrews, Scotland. Rule interpretations, and cases on which interpretations are based, comprise several volumes. Although beginners are encouraged to have access to and become familiar with the basic set of rules, it is not appropriate for the beginner to become burdened with all of the detailed rules of the game that are critical components of competitive golf. The beginner, in attempting to learn the basic strokes of the game, should be much more concerned about developing stroke techniques than whether or not a penalty stroke will be assessed to a player who moves the ball out of a depression or from behind a rock. Even as one moves from the beginner's stage, a somewhat liberal application of the rules may be employed as one plays alone or for social and recreational purposes with close friends. At these times the emphasis is not placed on keeping an absolutely correct score that will be used for determining a player's handicap or the winner or loser of a golfing competition.

Beginning the game. To initiate play the player must set the ball in the teeing area between two *markers* that have been provided for the purpose of identifying a specific part of the teeing area that is to be used. By using the markers as a guide, the ball may not be placed forward of an imaginary line running between the two markers nor more than two club lengths behind such an imaginary line. The ball may be placed directly on the ground (grass) or mounted on a small wood or plastic "tee." Any golf club that meets the specifications prescribed by the USGA may be used to strike the ball; thus, putting it "into play."

Touching the ball. According to the rules of the game, there are very few instances in which the player may touch the ball except with a legally specified club until the ball comes to rest on the "green", or putting surface. At that time a small marker (coin or other suitable flat object) may be placed behind the ball to mark its location. The ball can then be lifted, cleaned and held until it is the player's turn to putt the ball. The player then replaces the ball in front of the marker. There are several rules that relate to the "touching of a ball" after it has been put into play in the teeing area. For example, one may "lift, clean, and drop" a ball without penalty from an area of the course that has been designated "ground under repair." In addition, one can "pick up and drop" a ball that is determined to be unplayable. However, in this instance a penalty of one stroke will be incurred.

Putting rules. There are also rules that apply specifically to the putting green. For example, one may not straddle the imaginary line from the ball to the hole and execute a "croquet-type" stroke. In addition, a player who putts his/her ball in a manner that causes it to strike another player's ball on the putting service will be penalized two strokes. Therefore, a player is obligated to mark and lift his/her ball resting on the putting surface if it is reasonably close to the intended path of another player's ball. This particular rule applies only to balls that are stroked on the putting surface. No penalty would be incurred if a ball stroked from a location off the putting surface strikes a ball located on the putting surface. Even though no penalty would be assessed, the player whose ball was struck could replace the ball to its approximate location prior to the impact of the ball that was stroked onto the putting surface from off the green.

Scoring rules. As one completes the journey from teeing area to green and finishes the hole by stroking the ball into the cup, a tally of the number of strokes taken is made. This tally becomes the player's score on the hole. When this process is repeated either nine or eighteen times, the player has a score for a "half-round" or a full-round of golf. According to the rules of the game, a player must count a stroke for each of his/her efforts to propel the ball regardless of the distance the ball is moved. In fact, a stroke is charged when a deliberate swing is made even if the player "whiffs" or misses the ball entirely. As you might readily observe, a beginner who attempts to play a hole without instruction and practice might end up with a very large score if there were to be a strict and rigid application of the rules.

Course behavior and dress. In addition to formal rules there are a number of expectations which might be described as "appropriate behavior." These expectations relate to sportsmanship and genteel behavior. Even though these expectations are not carefully coded and reduced to formal statements of behavior, they have become a part of the culture of golf and have a surprising amount of uniformity throughout the golfing world. A few of these expectations are as follows:

a. One player does not make noise or movements that would distract another player who is ready to execute a stroke.

b. One player does not make derogatory or derisive remarks about another player during the course of the competition.

c. One player does not step on or near the intended path on which another player intends to stroke the ball on the putting surface.

d. A player does not place his/her feet close to the hole. (The preferred practice is to walk or stand no closer than arm's length as the flag stick is being removed from the cup.)

e. One player does not intentionally stand so that his/her shadow is cast on another player, the intended path of the ball, or the cup.

f. Players are expected to help partners and opponents alike in locating a ball that has rolled or bounced out of sight (e.g., high grass, bushes, holes, ditches).

g. When playing behind another group, it is expected that no player will execute a stroke until all members of the preceding group are clearly "out of range."

h. If you or your group are playing slowly and the group preceding you opens up a distance as great as one hole, you and/or your group should allow a group following you to "play through" if you or your group are slowing them down.

i. When a ball is "lost," you should limit your search to a maximum of five minutes before you officially declare the ball lost and put another ball into play.

j. After all players in your group have located their balls, you should quickly and efficiently decide on the club to be used and be ready to execute your stroke when it is your turn.

k. The player's turn to execute the next stroke is normally determined to be the player that is farthest from the hole. This player is said to be "away" and designated as the person who will take the next turn. The order of the play may become a safety factor when players are grouped in one area of the fairway. However, when players are on opposite sides of the fairway, the order of play is not critical. Often it can be agreed that the player who "gets ready first" goes ahead with the stroke.

l. On the putting surface the order of play is somewhat more rigidly applied since players must exercise care to avoid stepping on the surface on which another player's ball must roll.

7

m. Even though the player who is farthest from the cup on the putting surface putts first, the rules allow that player to continue putting until the ball is in the cup. It is expected, however, that the player will not exercise this right to "continuous putting" if it would be necessary for one or more of the player's feet to be on an area of the green across which another player's putt must roll. The practical consideration regarding the putting surface results from the fact that the imprint made from one's shoe on the putting surface remains as an indentation for several minutes. This imprint, even though relatively minor, can cause a slowly rolling ball to deviate from its path. Under normal circumstances this indentation will disappear in approximately five minutes which will leave the putting surface relatively free of indentations by the time the next group of players arrives on the putting surface.

n. When a player's ball impacts the putting surface from a relatively long distance or from a relatively steep trajectory, an indentation or "ball mark" will be made in the putting surface. It is expected that a player will repair this ball mark before continuing with play. Also, players are encouraged to repair other ball marks that might have been inadvertently left by others.

o. Golfers are expected to be "environmentally" sensitive. They are expected to appreciate the beauty of their surroundings, and they are expected to leave the course in as good or better condition than they found it. Therefore, limbs should not be broken and turf should not be left blemished. It is not unusual for a player's club to dislodge a small piece of sod as a stroke is made. However, it is incumbent upon the player to replace the piece of sod in a manner that would enable it to grow back and re-establish itself.

p. There is no standard dress code for the game of golf. However, there are local and regional as well as course specific expectations with which one should become familiar.

q. As a general rule, appropriate attire requires that swim suits and other abbreviated outfits be avoided. Further, it is expected that shoes and shirts will be worn.

As players become more familiar with the history and culture of the game, an increasing sensitivity to the game's tradition will be developed. As is true in life itself, there are aspects of the game that are not controlled by rigid directives. Players are expected to be guided by good sportsmanship and civility. In consideration of the wide variety of individuals who play the game of golf under many different conditions, it is surprising that such a high level of uniformity of conduct exists. This is a tribute to golfers everywhere who have developed an appreciation for the game and its traditions.

EQUIPMENT NEEDS

A standard set of golf clubs has nine irons, a putter and four woods. Even though the rules of golf permit the player to have 14 clubs, it is not necessary or even desirable for a beginner to invest in a full set of high quality golf clubs. A beginner can be well served with a partial set of used clubs for the initial learning experiences as the movements associated with the four basic strokes of golf are learned. In reality a beginner has little need for the number 1 wood or driver or the long irons—numbers 3, 2, or 1. In fact, the basic strokes of the game can be learned with one-half set of irons (9, 7, 5 or 8, 6, and 4), a pitching wedge, a putter and two or three woods (2, 3, 4; 3, 4, 5; or 3, 5, 7). The most critical factors regarding the "fit" of the

Pine Needles Learning Center
Pine Needles Resort
Southern Pines, NC

The Grand Cypress Academy of Golf
Grand Cypress Resort
Orlando, FL

beginner's club is to assure that the clubs are the appropriate weight and length, and that the clubs are appropriately gripped. Most any PGA professional can help you locate an appropriate "starter" set of clubs. Likewise, if the length of the clubs need to be adjusted or have new grips installed, this can be done at a very reasonable cost. (See Figure 1-1.)

Eventually, after you have learned to make the basic strokes and you have begun to make the motions involved in the various golf strokes in a consistent manner, you will want to go to an experienced PGA profes-

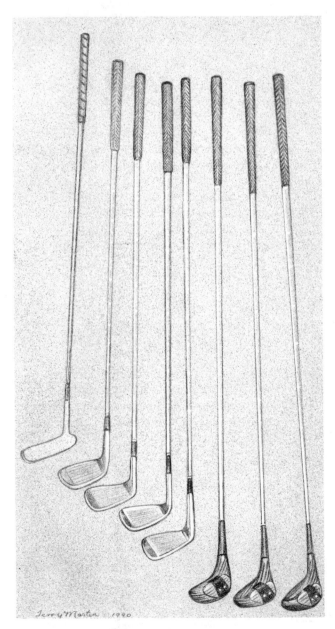

Fig. 1-1. A Beginner's Starter Set

sional and select a set of clubs that have the appropriate loft, lie, weight, and length for your height and arm length. Other factors such as the type of material from which the shaft is made and the size and appropriate material for the grip need to be determined. At some point in time you will want to make an investment in a set of clubs that are custom built for you. However, it is my judgment that this investment should be delayed until you have learned the basic fundamentals of the game and developed some measure of skill with the four basic strokes of golf. At that point in time you will be able to exercise good judgment in working with a professional or manufacturer in securing the right clubs for you.

Glove. A specially designed glove on the dominant hand (left for right-handed player) allows the club to be held more securely than with the bare hand. Also the glove will allow protection to the palm area next to the fingers. Very thin leather is used in order that feel and flexibility are maintained. Synthetic materials are also used to increase durability. These materials also do not get as slick as leather when wet.

Ball. For a beginner, there needs to be little concern for the type of ball used. There are many brands to choose from; however, the primary differences are in the type of cover and the way the inside of the ball is constructed. Until you become somewhat skilled, a two-piece ball or a ball with a cover made of surlyn that resists cutting when hit with the leading edge of an iron would be your best choice.

Golf balls that are manufactured with windings around a central core vary in hardness. This degree of hardness is referred to as *compression* which is the extent to which the ball can be deflected, or compressed, when a force is applied. The hardest is rated as 100 compression and the softest is rated as 80. Most beginners should use an 80 or 90 compression ball.

GLOSSARY OF TERMS

1. Birdie—One stroke less than the standard number of strokes or par taken to play a given hole.

2. Bogey—One stroke more than the standard number of strokes or par taken to play a given hole. Two strokes more than par on a hole is a double bogey and so on.

3. Eagle—Two strokes less than the standard or par taken to play a given hole.

4. Fairway—An area of grass that links the teeing area to the green. This area is defined by mowing the grass to a length of 1 1/2-2 inches. The expanse from teeing area to green may be interrupted by areas of rough, sand bunkers, water and other hazards.

5. Green—A carefully mowed area in which a cup or "hole" is located. There are 18 greens on a standard golf course. This area of closely cropped grass may be of differing size, shape and elevation; however, every effort is made to have the same type of grass cut to the same length on each green.

6. Handicap—A number used to represent the skill levels of individuals who play golf. An individual with a handicap of five is acknowledged as a more skillful player than one with a handicap of ten. The number has a direct relationship to a player's average score on an 18-hole course. The United States Golf Association (USGA) which establishes and interprets the rules of the game likewise delineate the rules of handicapping. This system allows players of differing skill levels to compete on a more comparable basis. Example: Player A with a handicap of 6 completes the 18-hole game or "round" with a total of 78 strokes; Player B with a handicap of 11 takes a total of 82 strokes; Player C with a handicap of 15 takes a total of 85 strokes. The net scores of Players A, B, and C respectively are 72, 71, and 70 on that day. Player A played his/her average round while players B and C played better than average. In fact, Player C's net score (gross score minus handicap) made him/her the winner. (Figure 0-1)

7. Hole—Refers to a playing area composed of teeing area, fairway, rough, hazards, sand traps and green. (Figure 0-2) A collection of 18 such configurations comprise a golf course. (Figure 0-3)

8. Loft—The angle between vertical and horizontal that the club's face is tilted. Loft is built into the club to cause the ball to become airborne. The amount of loft varies from the sand wedge which is tilted approximately 60 degrees from vertical to the putter which is vertical or 0-3 degrees loft.

9. Lie—The angle between the shaft and the bottom edge of the club head.

10. Lie—The position of the ball on the ground or other surface.

11. Neuromuscular—The central nervous system controls the body's muscles through signals from the brain.

12. Par—Standard or expected number of strokes needed to move the ball from teeing area onto the green and into the cup. A golf course is composed of a series of "holes" with a par of 3, 4, or 5 each. A standard 18-hole course has a comprehensive par of 70 to 72.

13. Rough—An area surrounding the fairway and green that contains grass that is typically allowed to grow to a length of 3" or more.

14. Target Line—An imaginary line running from the ball to the target. A player normally sets his/her body parallel to this line in an effort to move the club head on this line immediately before, during and after contacting the ball.

15. Tee—A wooden or plastic device that is stuck in the ground with a concave top that holds a golf ball.

16. Teeing Area—A defined grass area from which play is initiated. Markers are placed to further define the point from which the ball is placed to begin play on a given hole. The teeing area is often referred to as the "tee box" or simply as "the tee."

Hole	HDCP	1	2	3	4	5	6	7	8	9	Out
Gold		490	314	379	354	352	170	392	364	320	3135
Blue		480	309	359	345	338	143	363	352	307	2996
Silver		472	296	349	336	288	135	358	343	297	2874
Par		5	4	4	4	4	3	4	4	4	36
Handicap		2	16	6	10	12	18	4	8	14	
PLAYER A	6	6	4	5	4	4	3	5	4	4	39
PLAYER B	11	5	4	5	5	4	3	5	5	4	40
PLAYER C	15	6	4	5	5	5	3	5	5	5	43
Red (Ladies)		463	234	341	309	288	127	359	304	286	2711
Par		5	4	4	4	4	3	4	4	4	36
Handicap		2	16	4	8	12	18	6	10	14	

"When you replace the turf, you returf the place."

10	11	12	13	14	15	16	17	18	In	Total	
356	224	547	144	450	394	360	133	542	3150	6285	
349	208	529	132	460	367	320	118	522	3005	6001	
328	187	456	118	432	284	296	108	497	2706	5580	
4	3	5	3	4/5	4	4	3	5	35/36	71/72	
11	13	1	15	5	7	9	17	3			
4	3	6	3	6	4	4	3	6	39	78	72
5	3	6	3	6	5	5	3	6	42	82	71
5	4	5	4	6	5	4	3	6	42	85	70
273	121	446	81	377	230	250	100	418	2296	5007	
4	3	5	3	4	4	4	3	5	35	71	
7	13	1	17	5	11	9	15	3			

ATTEST

PLAYER

DATE

Fig. 0-1. Score Card With Handicap Examples

Fig. 0-2. Illustration of Golf Hole

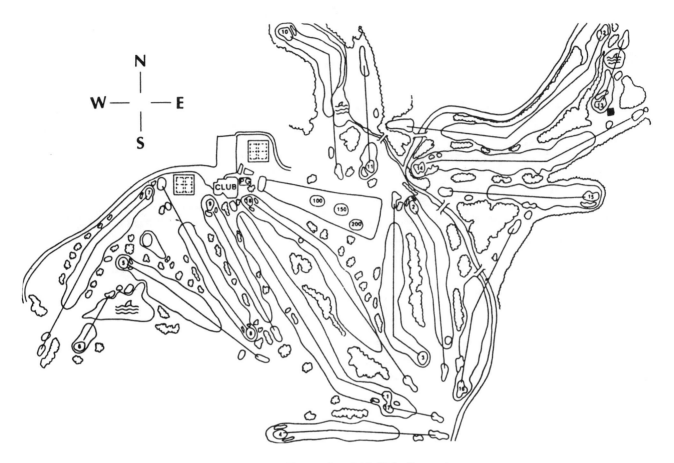

Fig. 0-3. Example of 18-Hole Layout

COMMANDMENTS OF GOLF

There are relatively few principles that have proved to be essential to successful execution of the basic strokes of golf. Through my interaction with professional golf instructors, as well as a considerable amount of teaching experience and study, these principles have been verified as "commandments." They are not to be taken lightly. In the chapters that follow, these essential principles or commandments will be shown in italics to emphasize their importance.

- On putts of 4' or less, listen for the ball to drop into the cup.

- Putts and chip shots require no wrist cocking or hinging. All other shots require that wrists cock and uncock.

- All strokes should accelerate through the ball and the club should not be allowed to decelerate prior to or upon impact.

- Try to see the club head strike the ball on all shots.

- The left elbow must be maintained in a relatively firm (not locked or rigid) position with minimum hinging action from address through impact.

- The knees must be slightly flexed at address and throughout the swing.

- Body posture and alignment enable a golfer to execute the basic mechanics of the golf swing. Likewise, poor posture or alignment may negate the use of proper swing techniques. Since you cannot observe your own posture and alignment, ask for help from others, use a video recorder or mirror when you are practicing.

1. The target line (the line on which you want the ball to travel) must be clearly established.

2. The clubface must be placed square or perpendicular to the target line.

3. The toes, hips, shoulders and eyes must be parallel to the target line at address.

4. After setting the body in a parallel position, the knees must be in a flexed position; the left elbow firm, the buttocks protruding, and the hands within 4" to 6" of the thigh line. This basic posture is appropriate for all shots. However, there is considerable variation among successful golfers with regard to posture and alignment for putting and chipping.

- The right leg must be at an angle of less than 90 degrees with the ground at address and during the swing.

- For the full swing the club head should be moved straight back from the ball and target for 6 to 12 inches with muscles of the upper left side of the chest and shoulder. After a distance of a few inches for the shorter clubs and a foot or so for the longer clubs, the body's (waist and shoulders) rotation should bring the club head inside the target line to a position opposite the right side as it moves upward.

- The speed of the backswing contributes little to the length of the shot; however, most high handicap players swing the club head back too rapidly and forward too slowly.

- Although individuals differ in the amount of time required to stop the backswing and initiate the forward swing, a moment is needed to make this transition. In this moment of transition the lower body (hips and legs) begins to move to the left (toward the target).

- The downswing is initiated with the feet and legs. As a result the arms will pull the club shaft back down to the same position it was in at address. As the downswing is initiated, the head remains relatively still. The preceding action requires coordination and good body mechanics for the lower body to shift to the left by the time the face of the club squares up to the target line.

- The length of the path or arc on which the club head travels, the speed of the club head and position of the club head at impact determine, in large part, the length of the shot made with a given club.

- The ball responds to the angle in which the face of the club strikes the ball. (See Figure 0-4.) The direction in which the club head travels at impact and the position of the clubface at impact determine the direction of the ball's flight.

BALL FLIGHT LAWS

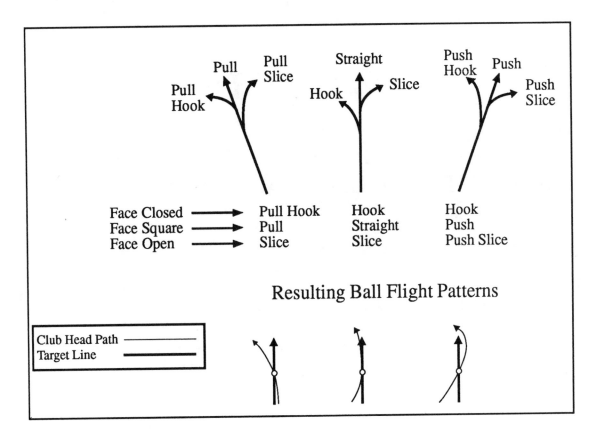

Fig. 0-4.   Club Face Position and Club Path

1.   When the clubface contacts the ball on a downward path, the angle of the face of the club will drive the ball upward.

2.   When the clubface is square to the target and is pulled on a path from outside the target line, the ball spins from left to right (clockwise).

3.   When the clubface is square to the target and moves on a path from inside the target line, the ball spins from right to left (counter clockwise).

4.   When the clubface moves on a path that is on the target line before, during and following impact, the ball moves forward on the same line.

CHAPTER 2

THE PHYSICAL
AND MENTAL FOUNDATION FOR THE GAME

The four strokes essential to the game of golf are built on a physical foundation that is unique to each individual. Each of us is a complex and unique blend of many mental, physical and emotional characteristics. Therefore, no two individuals are exactly the same although some sets of symbiotic twins have a large number of common characteristics.

It is important to acknowledge these individual differences as we engage in the processes of learning a new task and developing new skills. Some tasks will be learned more easily or more quickly by one person than another. One individual will have greater potential than another especially when it comes to psychomotor skill development. The ultimate level of psychomotor skill that one can achieve is determined by (1) the knowledge of techniques (nature and sequence of movements required, (2) body type (tall, short, thin, thick), (3) strength (hands, forearms, shoulders, back, thighs), (4) flexibility, (5) coordination (hand-eye), and (6) body mechanics (way in which body parts move in relation to each other, e.g. arms and legs). These are the variables that are responsible for your *physical foundation*.

This manual is written for the right-handed golfer; therefore, the illustration would have to be reversed if you elected to play the game left-handed. Likewise, all references to the hands, arms, feet and legs would be reversed for a left-handed player. Because nearly all golfers play the game right-handed, the majority of equipment and instructional publications are designed for right-handed players. The preceding factors cause me to encourage an adult beginner to play right-handed. To the novice it may be a bit confusing to define the right-handed golfer as one who stands on the left side of the line drawn from the ball to the target. It may also seem a bit strange to be told that the right-handed golfer's swing must be controlled by the left arm and hand. Nevertheless, this is true!

THE GOLF GRIPS

Your hands are your only contact with the golf club. Therefore, it is important to have a grip that allows you to maximize your physical foundation as you execute the golf swing. The three most common grips are the *overlapping*, the *interlocking*, the *side-by-side* or *baseball bat* grip and a variation used for the putting stroke. Some excellent players have used these different grips successfully which proves the point that no one grip is *right* for everyone.

Words alone are inadequate to convey physical positions and movements; therefore, the author's primary mode of communication will be through diagrams and illustrations. Words and phrases will be used primarily to emphasize especially important points. Even the word "grip" can be misleading if it suggests "squeezing." The club should be held lightly by the fingers. Tightly gripping the club tightens the forearm muscle and reduces its ability to move properly.

The Overlapping Grip. The first step in establishing your grip is to set the sole or bottom of the club head on the ground or other surface with the shaft inclined toward you. This is referred to as "soling the club." Lay the grip of the shaft diagonally across your left hand so that it can be held securely (not tightly) with the last three fingers of your left hand and the finger part of your palm, *not the middle of your palm.* (See Figure 2-1a.) While exerting light pressure, essentially by the fingers of the left hand, move the club a foot or two in all directions with the left arm to ensure that the first step has been made properly and the shaft is held securely.

The second step is initiated by placing the right hand under the left in a manner that allows the little finger of the right hand to *overlap* the extended knuckle of the first

finger of your left hand. The other fingers of your right hand should grip the club with the first finger of your right hand reaching down the shaft in a crooked or trigger position. (See Figure 2-1b.) With light finger pressure move the club back and forth and up and down to be certain that the club does not slip

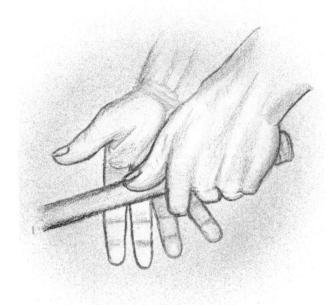

Fig. 2-1b. Right Hand Under Left; Little Finger of Right Overlaps the Extended Knuckle of the Left Hand

or twist. The key is to have enough pressure to keep the club from slipping; however, grip pressure that is too tight has a negative effect. (See Figures 2-1c.)

Regardless of the grip used the position of the knuckles as you look down on your hands is of vital importance. A neutral position which delivers the clubface square to the target line reveals two to three knuckles of the left hand while the "V" between the right thumb and forefinger points to your right ear. (See Figure 2-2a and 2-2b.)

Interlocking grip. All of the basic elements of the overlapping grip are present in the interlocking grip. The primary distinction relates to the position of the little finger of the right hand and the first finger

Fig. 2-1a. Shaft Diagonally Across Left Hand; Hold Securely With Last Three Fingers

17

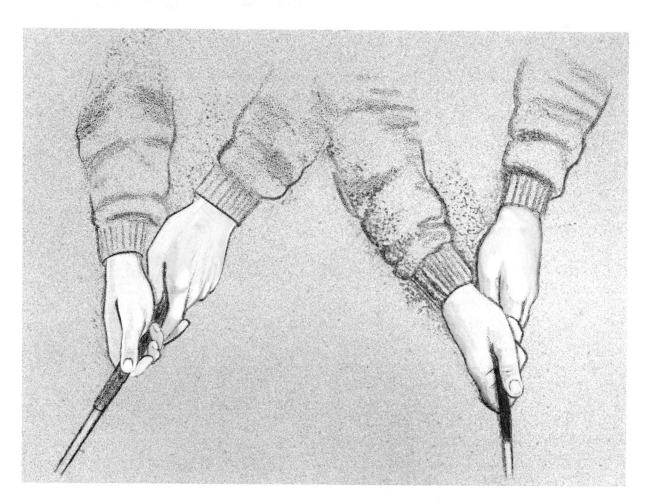

Fig. 2-1c. The Palm of the Right Hand Covers the Thumb of the Left Hand

of the left hand. In the overlapping grip, the little finger of the right hand "overlaps" the knuckle of the first finger of the left hand. In an effort to tie the two hands together more effectively, the interlocking grip links the little finger of the right hand and the first finger of the left hand. This interlocking of these two fingers and thus the interlocking of the hands gives this grip its name. (See Figure 2-3.) As mentioned previously, there have been successful professional golfers who have used both the interlocking and overlapping grips; therefore, there appears to be no real basis for concluding that one of these two grips is better than the other. It appears to be a matter of individual preference which may be affected as much by variables within an individual's physical foundation, e.g., size, shape, strength of hands and fingers. It is suggested that a beginner develop the overlapping grip and move toward the interlocking grip on an experimental basis if it appears that there would be an advantage to minimize the independence and dominance of either the right or left hand. Another advantage of the interlocking grip would be to increase the effectiveness of individuals with either small hands or limited hand strength by binding the hands together more as a single unit.

Side-by-side or baseball bat grip. The side-by-side grip is initiated in the same manner as the overlapping and interlocking in that the left hand is placed on the club first. The only distinct difference with the left hand position is that the left first finger is not pushed downward in a trigger-like shape on the club shaft. Instead, all four fingers of the left hand are touching and

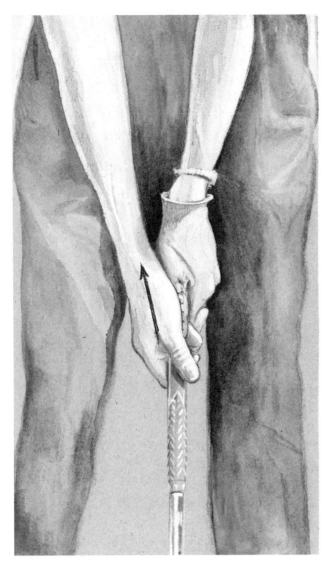

Fig. 2-2a. The Right Thumb and Forefinger Form a "V" Shape

pressed together, and the left thumb is extended down the shaft. As the right hand is placed on the club shaft, all four fingers are touching the shaft with the little finger of the right hand pressed tightly against the first finger of the left hand. If the club is held in the manner described, it is clearly a "side-by-side" grip with much of the control in the fingers of the two hands rather than the palms of the two hands. (See Figure 2-4.) If one allows the club shaft to rest more in the palms of the two hands, the grip takes on a somewhat different character more akin to the gripping of a baseball bat.

The side-by-side grip is used successfully by very few professional players, and it is judged to be an inferior grip for the vast

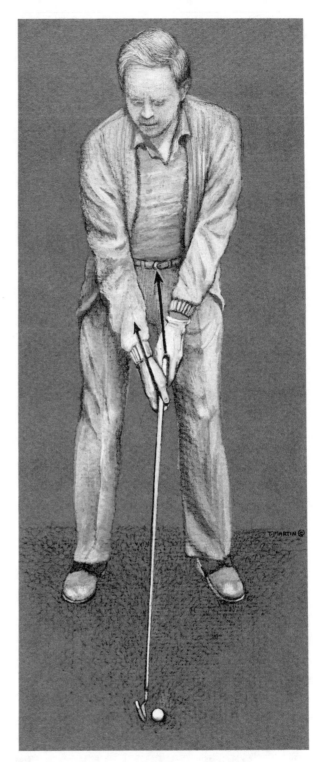

Fig. 2-2b. The "V" of the Right Hand Points to Right Ear; The "V" of the Left Points at Chin

majority of players. This grip tends to lead the player to rely too much on hand action and less on the shoulders and arms for the golf swing. Individuals who have limited strength may feel more comfortable in the early stages of the learning process with the club held more securely like a baseball bat.

19

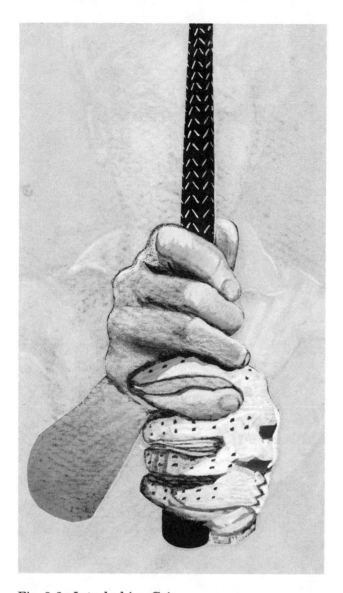

Fig. 2-3. Interlocking Grip

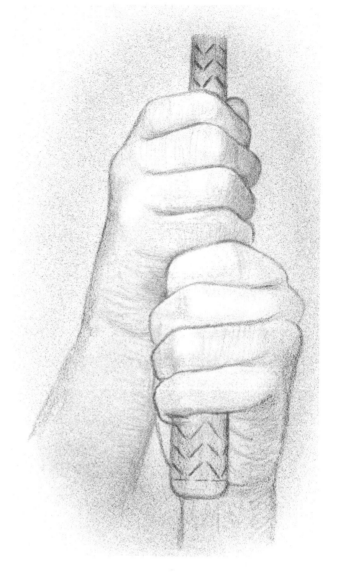

Fig. 2-4. Side-by-Side Grip

Even for these individuals, the primary gripping pressure must be in the fingers rather than in the palms of the hands. Individuals who have played a considerable amount of baseball or softball may feel that this is a more "normal" grip. However, for most individuals learning the game of golf, the side-by-side, or baseball bat, grip should be viewed as a transition toward the overlapping or interlocking grip. The sooner it is realized that the baseball swing and the golf swing are different, the better off they will be in developing an effective golf swing. With the understanding that the two swings are different and a realization that the golf club and baseball bat are designed differently, it

becomes obvious that a different grip is required.

The putting grip. As you will learn, the putting game is, in reality, a "game within a game." Many elements of the putting game are unlike the elements of the game that take the player from the tee through the fairway or the rough onto the green. One of the differences in the putting game is the variation in either the overlapping or the interlocking grip with the palms of the two hands facing each other and the back of the left hand on a line perpendicular to the target line. There are about as many variations of the putting grip, alignment, and posture as there are golfers. However, it is best if one begins with a basic or standard grip and posture. In this way you will know the point from which the variation is made. The variation that is most frequently adopted in the putting grip is that the forefinger of the left hand extends down across the fingers of the right hand, or the forefinger of the right hand is placed down the shaft of the putter to provide a player with more control or "feel" as the putting stroke is made. (See Figure 2-5.)

THE STANCE

In establishing the physical foundation for the golf swing, the grip and the stance are the two major variables that can be determined by you, the player. Some instructors refer to grip and stance as the *static* part of the golf swing. As previously

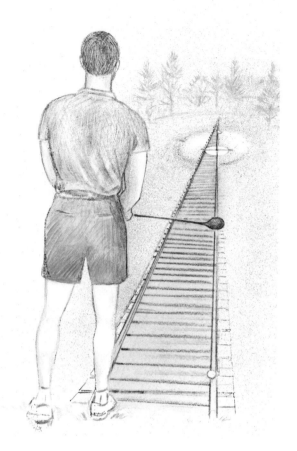

Fig. 2-6a. Square Alignment of Body to Target Line; Toe Line Parallel to Target Line

mentioned, a number of the other variables in the physical foundation such as body type, strength, flexibility, coordination and body mechanics, are somewhat predetermined and can be altered only to a very limited degree. After you have learned the mechanical aspects of gripping the club, attention must then be focused on the physical aspects of the stance which determines the body's relationship to the ball and the target. In reality, the combination of grip and stance predetermine, in a major way, the manner in which the club can be swung. Understanding and repeating the fundamentals related to grip and stance allows you to establish a pre-stroke routine that works for you. Consistency is a positive outcome of having a routine way in which you place your hands on the club and take your stance.

Fig. 2-5. Modified Grip for Putting

21

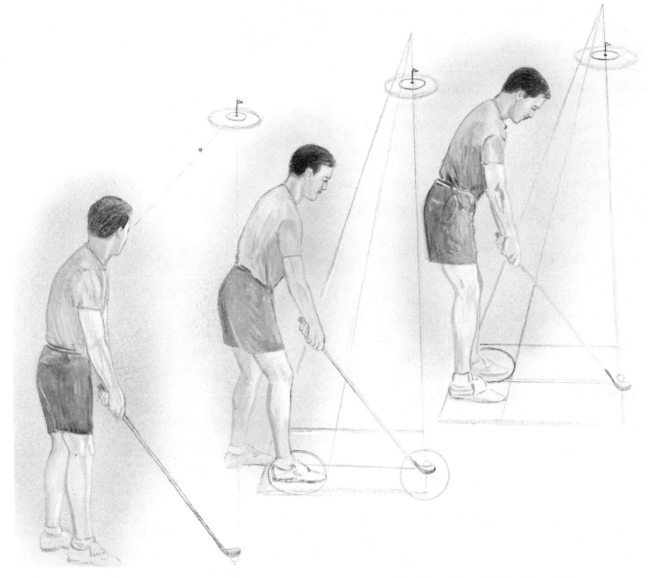

Fig. 2-6b. Square Alignment of Body to Target Line; Toe Line Parallel to Target Line

Alignment. After you have gripped the club properly, you then, without concern for placing the feet (except that a right-hand player should stand to the left of a line that extends through the ball to the target), *place the face of the club behind the ball and perpendicular to the line extending through the ball to the target (the target line).* This first step, establishing the target line, in the alignment process is extremely important. Unfortunately, this is a step that is overlooked or accomplished improperly by a large majority of beginning and high handicap golfers. After the club has been placed in proper alignment to the target, *your body (toes, waist and shoulders) must be set parallel to an imaginary line running through the ball to the target (the target line).* (See Figures 2-6a-b.) One of the easiest ways for you to establish an imaginary line through the ball to the target is to set the ball on the ground with the label (insignia) of the ball pointing toward the target. With the body (toes, hips, shoulders, and eyes) parallel to an imaginary target line, a perpendicular, or 90 degree relationship is then established from the ball to you. (See Figures 2-7a-b.) The basic alignment position in relation to the ball is to have the ball centered on your body. Therefore, if the golf club is positioned

Fig. 2-7a. Ball Positioned Perpendicular to Player's Body

behind the ball facing the target, the shaft of the club will be pointing toward the inside of your left leg. (See Figure 2-8.) While these basic principles of alignment are very logical to discuss and illustrate, it may be difficult for a beginner to establish these imaginary parallel and perpendicular alignment lines without aids or an observer. Although aids and observers cannot be used in an actual game of golf, they can and should be used in the process of learning and practicing. Alignment is fundamental to a proper stance; a proper stance is essential to establishing good balance, the physical foundation for an effective golf swing. Ball position is another important factor; however, since ball position varies with each of the four strokes, it will be discussed and illustrated in Chapters 3 through 9.

Posture. Once the grip and the alignment have been established, there are

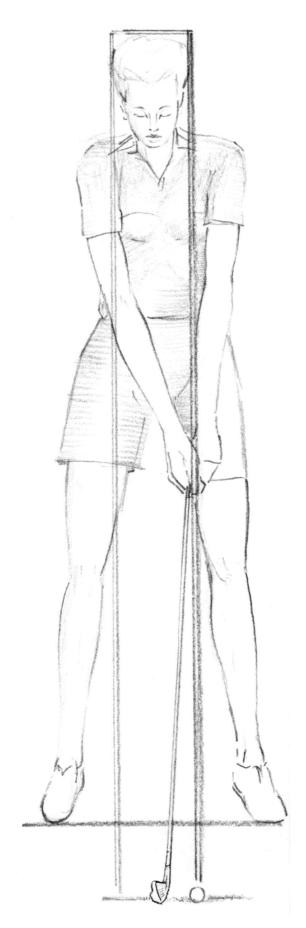

Fig. 2-7b. Ball Positioned Perpendicular to Player's Body

23

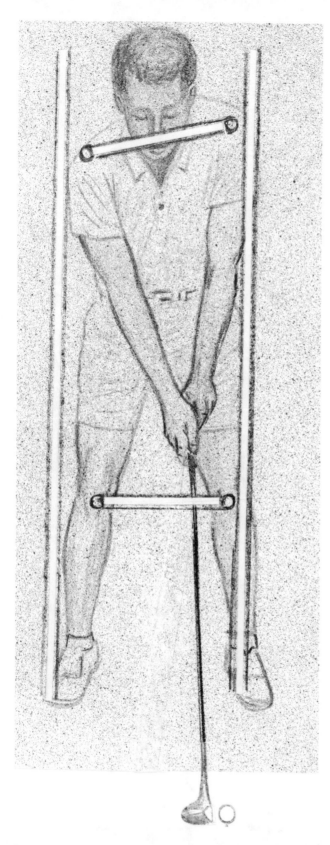

Fig. 2-8. Left Arm as an Extension of Club Shaft Inclined Above Inside of Left Thigh

certain body positions that further determine the proper stance. *The posture is determined by the angular relationships of the parts of the body (arms, back, thighs, knees) to the shaft of the club and the distance of a player's body from the golf ball.* The several key body positions and relationships are as follows:

- The right-handed golfer's left shoulder is held slightly higher than the right shoulder.

- *With the arms hanging down naturally, the player's left arm is held in a relatively firm, not rigid, position which becomes basically an extension of the shaft of the golf club.* (Review Figure 2-8.)

- While a golfer's body type may determine to some extent the up and down relationship of the line between the golfer's left shoulder and the club shaft, the other dimension of the line running between the golfer's left shoulder and ball must be reasonably straight. (As illustrated, avoid rigidity or extremes in the up/down variation of this line.) Although a description of the several elements involved in a player's posture are being discussed separately, it should be recognized that these posture elements are interrelated and some of them are established simultaneously. Just as it is important to avoid rigidity in the relationship of a player's back, thighs and knees. *The knees need to be flexed but not bent excessively.* The appropriate amount of flex or bend of the knees can be judged somewhat by sighting down past the kneecaps to the top of the shoes.

- Simultaneously, *a golfer needs to bend forward from the hips with the spine in a straight but angular line with the ground as illustrated. In establishing this part of the posture, a player's posterior noticeably protrudes backward.* (See Figure 2-9.)

24

Grand Cypress Resort
Orlando, FL

Vintage Golf Schools
Port Royal Golf Club
Hilton Head Island, SC

Fig. 2-9. Angular Relationship of Knees, Hips, and Back

- The positioning of the knees, back and posterior creates distinct angles for the lower and upper legs that control the body's balance throughout the golf swing.
- The position of a player's head in relation to the other parts of the body and the position of the ball are important features of a player's posture. If one were to draw a line from a right-handed player's left cheek to the back of the ball, this would help to fix the ball/head relationship. As a general principle, a player's head remains relatively still and in a distinctly "behind the ball" position. There is a general tendency for beginners, and even experienced golfers, to allow the head to move back and forth excessively. They are often admonished to "keep your head still."

The principle of "relatively still and behind the ball" is sound; however, a rigid adherence to this principle might cause individuals to be "too stiff" and not sufficiently *fluid* in terms of their body mechanics. (Review Figure 2-8.) There is also a tendency among beginners and high handicap golfers to lift and jerk their head and shoulders to the left during the downward part of the golf swing. This tendency often brings about the admonition to "keep your head down". This admonition frequently causes beginners and high handicap players to lower the chin and tuck it almost to the point of touching the chest. A much better admonition would be to: *keep your chin up and your eye on the ball during the golf swing.* Keeping the head relatively still with a minimum left-to-right or up-and-down movement allows a much more consistent execution of the golf swing. There will be some natural head movement; however, excessive head movement leads to inconsistency in stroking the ball. A greater understanding of the importance of these posture elements will be gained as you begin to execute the dynamic or moving part of the golf swing as described and illustrated in Chapter 6.

PHYSICAL CONDITIONING

As indicated previously, your ultimate level of skill development will be determined by several physical variables that can be altered by exercise and body conditioning. Strength of certain muscles and flexibility are important to your success in executing the basic strokes of golf, especially the full swing. Obviously your general level of health and fitness is the foundation upon which a specific program of conditioning for golf should be built. Good nutrition and a regular program of exercise such as walking two or three miles every other day, low impact aerobics, or vigorous swimming for 30 minutes three or four times per week are the basics for your conditioning program. Remember that a physician should be consulted before beginning any conditioning program.

Trunk rotation. Individuals who are thick through the waist have more difficulty getting sufficient body rotation to make an effective full swing than those who are thin. However, trunk rotation exercises will increase anyone's flexibility which is so important to a golfer's ability to wind and unwind the upper body. To begin the trunk rotation exercise, stand erect with feet close together. Place the grip of the club against the upper chest and hold the shaft with both hands as the arms are outstretched. (See Figure 2-10.) Turn a few inches to the right and then a few inches to the left. This exercise should be repeated as you gradually increase the range of your rotation. Your objective is to be able to have your belt buckle facing the target on the forward swing and your back facing the target on the back swing. This exercise should be done slowly with 10 to 20 repetitions several times each day.

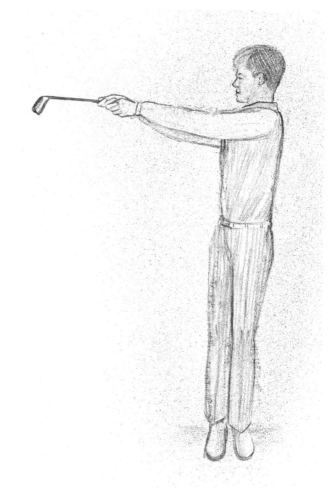

Fig. 2-10. Trunk Rotation

Hamstring stretch. The large muscle in the back of the upper leg needs conditioning for both endurance and liveliness. One of the most common ways to condition the hamstring muscles to sit on a bench or on the floor with one leg extended outward in front of you. The other leg will be bent comfortably to your side. Now slowly lean forward until you feel a stretching sensation in the back of thigh of your extended leg. Hold this position for a count of five. (See Figure 2-11.) With your chin up and your back straight, hold this position for a count of ten. Sit up straight and repeat the stretch again, but do not bounce. After several repetitions, shift your position with the other leg extended outward and repeat the stretching exercise.

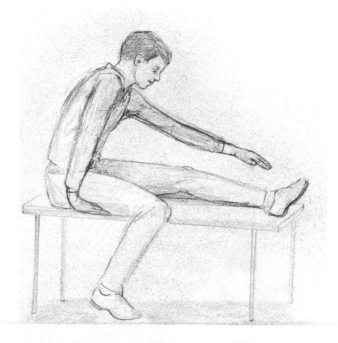

Fig. 2-11. Hamstring Stretch

26

Calf stretch. The large muscle on the back of the lower leg surrounds and supports the Achilles tendon. These calf muscles and tendon can be conditioned by stretching. Stand approximately 24 to 30 inches from a solid wall and lean with outstretched arms and hands against the wall. (See Figure 2-12.) The forward leg should be bent at the knee with the foot flat on the floor. The back leg should be straight with the foot flat on the floor. By bending your arms, slowly lean forward until you feel a stretching sensation in the back of the calf. Hold this position for a count of five. Repeat several times; then reverse front and back legs.

Fig. 2-13. Side Bend

Fig. 2-12. Calf Stretch

Side bend. To increase flexibility of the muscles down your sides, stretching is necessary. Stand erect with feet close together and hold a golf club over your head by grasping each end. Then bend as far one way as you can; straighten up and bend the other way. (See Figure 2-13.) Repeat the bending ten times in each direction.

Grip. To strengthen the hands for a more secure grip use hand springs or squeeze a rubber ball. Repeat the squeezing action until fatigue sets in or you feel a burning sensation. Caution: Do not exercise the hands and forearms excessively the same day you plan to practice the golf swing or play golf.

Wrists and forearms. Although several devices are marketed to help you condition the wrists and strengthen the forearms, a simple device can be made from a 15-inch round wooden dowel or part of a broom stick, a 36-inch piece of string and a 3 to 5 pound weight. Tie one end of the string to the middle of the wooden rod and the other to the weight. Hold the wooden rod at each end and extend your arms straight out in front of you. (See Figure 2-14.) By twisting the rod, wind the string around the wooden rod. Your forearms will be strengthened by alternately raising and lowering the weight.

The wrist curl can also be used to strengthen the forearm. For this exercise support the forearms on a table with the hand (palm up) extending over the edge. Using a small weight or hammer, lower the hand downward as far as possible, then curl it up as far as possible. Hold in each position for a count of five.

Shoulder stretch. To strengthen and increase the flexibility of the shoulders and upper back muscles, there are two exercises that can be helpful if performed on a frequent and regular basis. The first of these is simply to extend your left arm as far as possible to the right without rotating your waist. You may want to support and pull the arm gently to get full extension. (See Figure 2-15.) Then do the same thing with the right arm by extending it across your body to the left.

For the second exercise, stand erect with your arms at your sides. Then raise first one arm and then the other directly away from your side and upward to a vertical position while keeping your elbow straight. To build strength, hold a hammer or small weight in your hand as you lift the arm. (See Figure 2-16.)

THE MENTAL SIDE OF GOLF

Even though the physical movements included in golf have a direct influence on the ball, your knowledge and your emotions play an important role in the execution of stroke mechanics and your resulting enjoyment of the game. Therefore, it is important for you to let your mind and emotions work for you and not against you as you learn and play the game of golf.

As mentioned in the first part of this chapter, golf for you as an adult beginner is a game to be enjoyed. Of course you want to play well; however, too frequently, adults

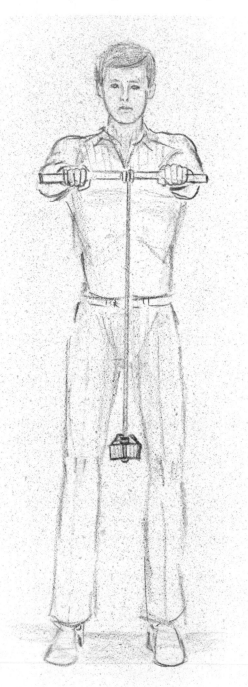

Fig. 2-14. Wrist and Forearm Exercise

28

Fig. 2-16. Arm Raise

Fig. 2-15. Shoulder Stretch

expect "too much too soon," and as a result they become impatient and frustrated with their imperfection. It is important to condition your mind in a positive way as you learn and play the game. Make learning and practicing fun. Set reasonable, yet achievable goals. Study the techniques, get instruction, and practice. (See Chapter 10.) Tension disrupts the smooth execution of stroke techniques. Enjoy the process. Do not place so much pressure on your drive for success, perfection, score or winning that you cannot relax and enjoy yourself. Realize that tour professionals who make millions of dollars during their careers do not achieve perfection in the game of golf. They have physical, mental, and emotional shortcom-

ings just like the rest of us. We only differ by the extent of our imperfections; but, we do not depend on the game for our livelihood either!

Your mind's impact on learning. Learning to play golf involves the mind and the emotions as well as the muscles. The neurons in the brain control memory, physical movements and our feelings. The human mind functions through two hemispheres of "grey matter" in the area between our ears that we call a brain. Each side or hemisphere has its own special functions which influence our learning, our thinking, and our behavior. The game of golf requires the involvement of both hemispheres. Coop, Wiren and Sheehen, authors of *The New Golf Mind*, contend that "golf may be unique among sports in the degree of participation and cooperation it demands of each hemisphere."*

You may be aware that the left hemisphere of the brain controls the right side of the body, and the right hemisphere controls the left side of the body. However, the technical aspects of the brain's processing of neurons is not of concern as we consider its impact on learning and playing golf. For purposes of our discussion, it is important to recognize that our left and right hemispheres perform different functions.

The left hemisphere, for convenience of discussion, has been labeled by Coop et al. as the brain's *ANALYZER* which controls most of our rational, critical, step-by-step thinking. The functions of verbalizing, deducing, computing, calculating, speaking, writing, reading, and ordering are all controlled primarily through the *ANALYZER*. (See Figure 2-17.)

The right hemisphere has been labeled as the *INTEGRATOR*. It specializes in the creative and artistic side of our being as it keeps us in touch with our feelings and emotions. The *INTEGRATOR* directs our intuition rather than our analytical processes. It helps us visualize, gain insight, and orient ourselves in relationship to our environment. Motor skill performance such as diving and gymnastics are highly dependent on the *INTEGRATOR*.

Coop et al., in *The New Golf Mind*, treat this subject extensively and cite research studies and in other ways document the validity of the "split brain." Our concern here, as you begin to learn the game of golf, is to introduce you to the complex process of motor learning in a manner which will allow you to use your mind as a positive force.

The drawing of the two hemispheres shown in Figure 2-18 shows the special golfing faculties of the *ANALYZER* (left) and the *INTEGRATOR* (right) of your brain. Your awareness of these functions and the way

your brain receives, processes, and sends signals can help you learn, practice, and play more effectively. For example, you should be able to recognize your own left or right brain dominance. Your dominance is not good or bad per se. However, it will definitely affect the way you learn, practice, and play. You need both hemispheres to achieve your full potential. Therefore, you may need to recognize the benefits from your less dominate hemisphere and cultivate these faculties. It will be interesting for you to observe and interact with others who are like you or different in terms of hemisphere dominance.

It is especially important that the instructor you choose be reasonably well balanced with a strong left brain orientation. A professional golfer may be quite successful with right hemisphere dominance; however, teaching and learning require analysis, attention to detail, and step-by-step processing. This manual is written from a strong left brain orientation; nevertheless, I recognize the importance of "feel," "touch," and "tempo" in the execution of each of the four strokes of golf. In the development of psychomotor skill, it is essential to (1) know the proper movements of a technique, (2) perform the movements correctly, although more slowly than ultimate performance, and (3) repeat and increase the speed until the movements become a thoroughly established habit. The *ANALYZER* is essential in the first two steps in psychomotor skill development. The *INTEGRATOR* needs to be brought into steps two and three to bring harmony into the otherwise rigid or mechanical movements.

During the actual playing of the game of golf, the *INTEGRATOR* serves as synthesizer and executor. The right hemisphere translates the relevant analytical information from the left hemisphere into non-verbal and non-critical language of its own. The *INTEGRATOR* then permits the body to

*Excerpted from the book, *The New Golf Mind*. Permission Golf Digest/Tennis, Inc.—Copyright (c) 1978.

THE TWO-SIDED BRAIN: GENERAL FUNCTIONS

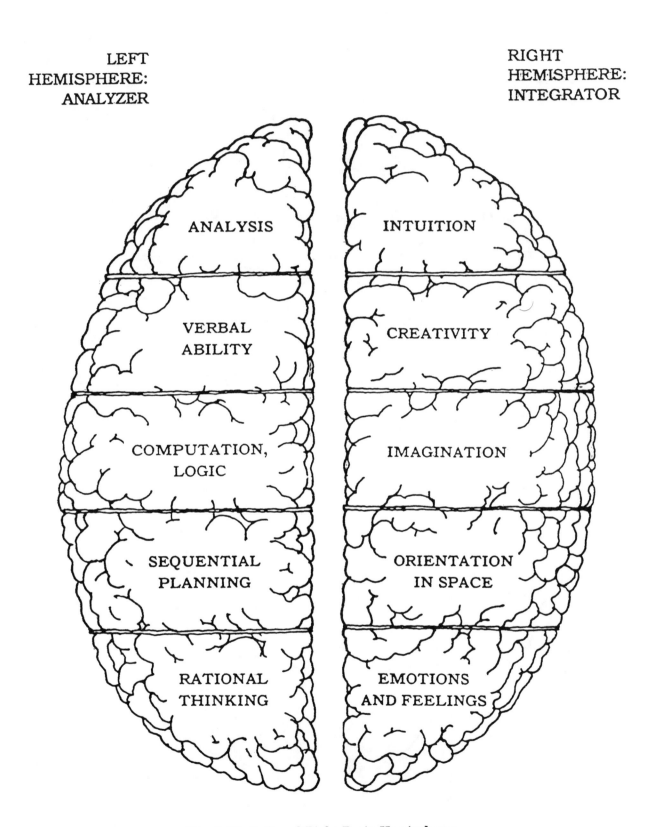

LEFT
HEMISPHERE:
ANALYZER

RIGHT
HEMISPHERE:
INTEGRATOR

ANALYSIS

INTUITION

VERBAL
ABILITY

CREATIVITY

COMPUTATION,
LOGIC

IMAGINATION

SEQUENTIAL
PLANNING

ORIENTATION
IN SPACE

RATIONAL
THINKING

EMOTIONS
AND FEELINGS

Fig. 2-17. Left and Right Brain Hemispheres

THE TWO-SIDED BRAIN: GOLF FUNCTIONS

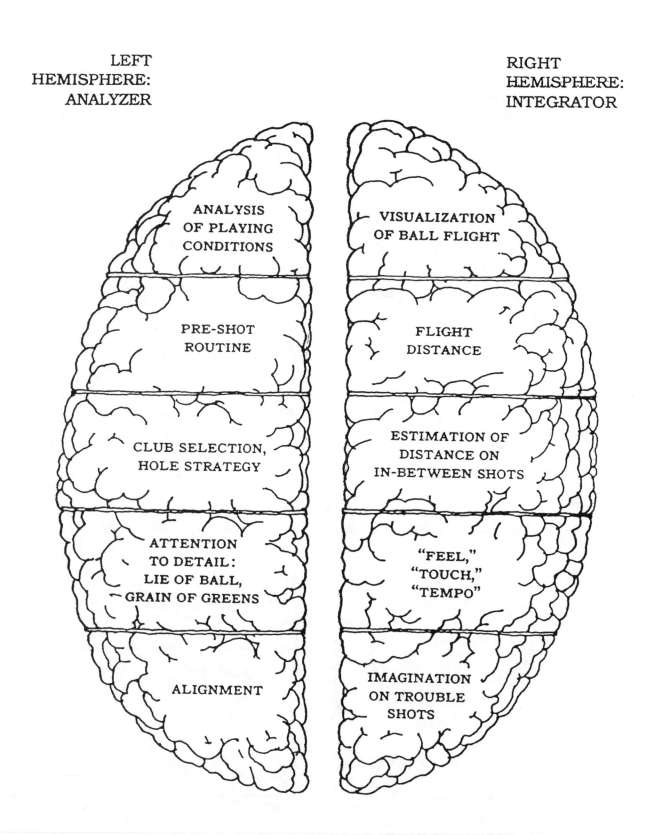

Fig. 2-18. Functions of Each Hemisphere and Relationship to Golf

execute the swing unimpaired by conscious thought or detail. This switch from *ANALYZER* to *INTEGRATOR* must be made for successful execution of the golf stroke. The full swing especially happens too fast for you to "think your way" through the swing. You may hear the phrase, "paralysis through analysis" used to describe the inability to integrate the movements necessary to swing with freedom and tempo.

Most of us have had split-brain interference. For example, when you become excited you may notice that you have difficulty choosing the correct words or speaking them clearly. The verbal skills located in the left hemisphere are being blocked by the emotions of the right hemisphere. An opposite, but equally frustrating problem, is encountered by typists who try to comprehend the content they are typing. The left brain's analytical process will block the right brain's integration of movements and thus reduce a typist's words-per-minute rate.

Putting, described in Chapter 3, is a good example in the game of golf where each hemisphere plays a different although equally important role. To execute a putting stroke of 25 feet, your *ANALYZER* must evaluate the putting surface e. g., does the surface slope uphill, downhill, from left to right or right to left. Then the *INTEGRATOR* must convert this information for you to sense or feel the force and direction of your stroke. Both hemispheres must be used to give you the best chance of rolling the ball into the cup. To ignore needed input related to the condition and contour of the surface would be just as foolish as failing to allow your hand-eye coordination and sense of touch to assist you in moving the putter back and forth the correct distance to roll the ball into the cup. Using both hemispheres is essential if you are to reach your potential.

In golf the pre-stroke activities such as choice of club, grip, alignment, ball position, and posture need the control of the *ANALYZER*. Once the mind has gathered and processed the necessary pre-stroke information, the INTEGRATOR must be allowed to take over and execute the stroke. Only one or two "in-swing" thoughts e. g., "See the club head strike the ball" or "Pause at the top" can be allowed without adverse interference.*

*Excerpted from the book, *The New Golf Mind*. Permission Golf Digest/Tennis, Inc.—Copyright (c) 1978.

CHAPTER 3

THE PUTTING GAME

After establishing the physical foundation for the four basic strokes of the game of golf, one must begin the process of skill development related to each of the basic strokes. As a professional teacher, I recognize the importance of the principles of "simple to complex, starting with the basics, early success, correct body mechanics, and repetition" as they relate to skill development. Consistent with these principles, I recommend that you begin your journey to "a lifetime of golfing enjoyment" by developing a putting stroke and an understanding of the *putting game.*

In chapter 2, as the putting grip was described, reference was made to the "game within a game." The reference to "a game within a game" while not technically accurate, does emphasize the significant role of putting in determining a player's score. Also, the putting stroke is quite unique among the four basic strokes in that the putting stroke is designed to roll the ball while all other strokes are designed to cause the ball to become airborne. If you recall the brief description of the game provided in Chapter 1, the standard expectation on each hole regardless of its length and its *par* is that two putting strokes will be used. Therefore, on a standard 18-hole course, 36 putting strokes are anticipated. To place the importance of putting into perspective, just consider the fact that one-half of the expected "points" or

"score" is determined by one type of skill. It follows logically that one must give considerable attention to this type of skill, i.e. putting. Unfortunately, many beginners and high handicap players never receive instruction on "the putting game" and seldom practice the few techniques that they may have learned during the process of playing the game. One of the primary reasons for this unfortunate circumstance results from a typical player's preoccupation with the full swing using long irons, fairway woods and the driver.

Another reason that putting is not taught is the mistaken assumption that putting is all "feel"—an art that has no real technical qualities. As a professional educator, I certainly recognize human variation in visual acuity, depth perception, tactile facility, hand-eye coordination, as well as brain hemisphere dominance which effect skill development and determine to a large extent the ultimate level of performance. However, certain scientific principles do affect the putting process. As a result, the process can be and has been analyzed. Certain fundamental principles have been identified, and these principles can be taught and learned. By understanding and applying these basic fundamentals even the most "feel-oriented" and right brain dominant person will have a more consistent and effective putting game. Obviously an analytical left brain dominant person will be more secure with some fundamentals (rules) to guide learning and performance.

As indicated previously, under regular circumstances the ball may be "lifted" and "cleaned" only on the putting surface after it is put into play from the teeing area (tee or tee box). The correct method of marking the location of the ball is to place a coin or other thin flat object directly behind the ball. After others who are further away from the cup have putted, you can replace your ball by setting the ball in front of the coin or marker.

THE MECHANICS OF THE PUTTING STROKE

After learning to grip the putter properly, a player assumes a basic or standard posture as described in Chapter 2. Although it is acknowledged that putting can be done successfully from a greater variety of positions than any of the other basic strokes, you need to learn the standard or basic approach from which you, as an individual, may vary.

Alignment. As with other strokes, the blade of the club (putter) must be perpendicular to the target line. A line on the putter head perpendicular to the clubface helps in the alignment process. If the contour of the putting surface (green) is level and the ball can be rolled on a straight line to the cup (hole), the putter will be perpendicular to an imaginary line pointed directly at the cup (target). (See Figure 3-1.) However, a surface that slopes left or right will require a target line that is left or right of the cup. (See Figure 3-2a.)

In this circumstance the ball stroked on the target line will start on the target line and then, as it loses speed, it will curve right or left depending on the contour of the surface of the green. (See Figure 3-2b.) Deciding the target line is the first step in putting. This step is often referred to as "reading the green." Judging the amount of slope and the

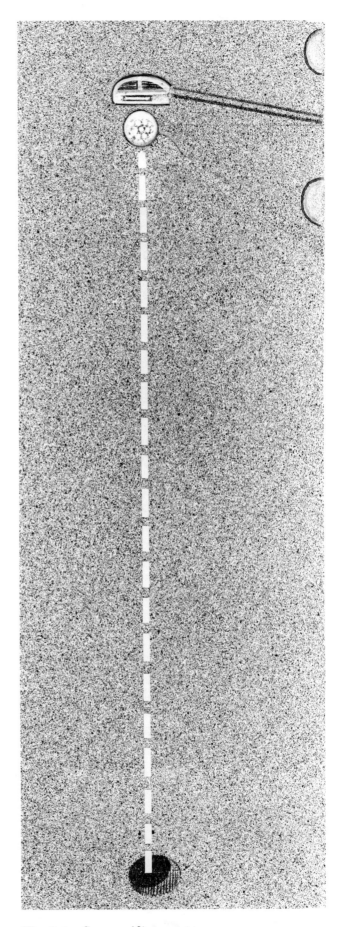

Fig. 3-1. Square Alignment

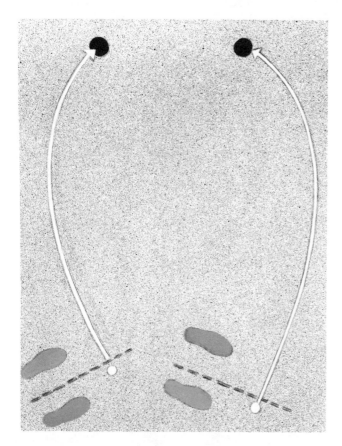

Fig. 3-2a. Alignment on Sloping Green

Fig. 3-2b. On Sloping Green the Ball Moves From Target Line in Direction of Slope

distance from the ball to the cup is crucial to successful putting. Your judgement will improve with experience if approached systematically and consistently. View the target line (line) by looking at the surface on which the ball is to travel from a vantage point behind the ball looking toward the hole. It may also be helpful to view the line from a vantage point across the green with the cup between you and the ball. Take care not to walk or stand on the line of other players. Determining the target line should be done efficiently to avoid slowing down other players.

After determining the target line and after others who had longer putts have putted, you should replace your ball. Tip: When placing the ball in front of your coin or marker, place the surface of the ball with the manufacturer's label on top and on the intended target line. This position of the ball helps you to set the putter blade perpendicular to the label and the target line. (See Figure 3-3.)

Posture. With the club properly gripped, your body aligned, and the feet parallel and approximately 9-12" from the target line, *the knees should be flexed,* the center of gravity lowered, and the upper body tipped slightly forward. As illustrated in Figure 3-4, this position should allow your eyes to be directly above the ball and the target line. The arms and the chest form a triangle as the hands grip the putter and the player bends forward in the putting stance. The long sides of the triangle (upper arms) should not be extended rigidly or straight. Instead, the elbows should bend naturally and comfortably.

The Putting Stroke. As mentioned previously, there are more successful variations of the putting stroke than any of the other four basic strokes of golf. The purpose of this PRIMER is to provide you with a relatively simple, "no frills" approach to the putting stroke. As you gain experi-

36

Fig. 3-3. Using Ball Label to Assure Direction

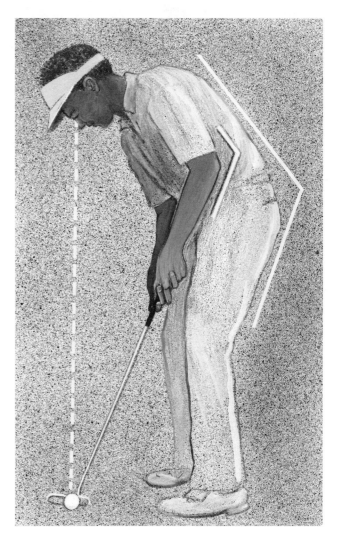

Fig. 3-4. Body and Head Position

ence, you may want to experiment with one of a variety of techniques that successful golfers have found to work well for them. The basic putting stroke recommended for a beginning golfer is an extension of the parallel and perpendicular or "square" approach established in the previous sections on alignment and posture. After you have (1) gripped the putter properly and lightly, (2) established the target line, and (3) aligned your body to that target line, the left shoulder and arm should push the putter away from the ball on an extension of the imaginary target line. You must determine the distance to push the putter away, or back from, the ball to generate sufficient putter head speed to roll the ball to the cup. After the putter head has been moved straight back the desired distance on the target line, both arms should move the putter head back

down the imaginary target line striking the ball and rolling it toward the cup. As illustrated in Figure 3-5, it is important to keep the left wrist straight with no hinging as the arms go back or forward.

The judgement involved in taking the putter away from the ball and the speed with which the putter head is returned on the target line through the ball determines how fast the ball will roll. Your judgement with regard to these two factors is referred to as "feel." This human quality separates putters into skill levels from "excellent" to "awful"! While any golfer can be taught the mechanics of alignment and posture, the "feel" for the length and speed of the stroke is an individual quality that can be developed or improved with practice. Holding the club lightly

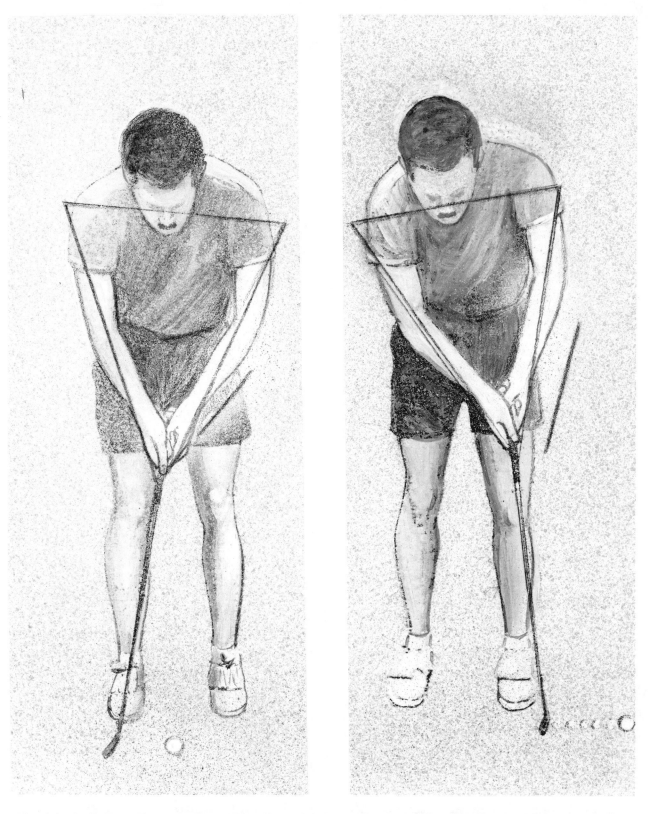

Fig. 3-5. Left Wrist Remains Firm Throughout Stroke as the Two Sides of the Triangle are Maintained

in your fingers will allow you to develop better feel than a tight grip that causes tenseness in your forearm muscles. However, this individual quality is similar to other human qualities such as hand/eye coordination, visual acuity and artistic talent in that they are possessed in different degrees by individuals. It may be helpful to give yourself some guidelines for distance. Depending on the weight of your putter, the type of grass on the putting surface and the length of the grass, the ball will be rolled a given distance by the length of your back and forward stroke of the putter. For example, you may find that a five-inch backward and forward stroke will roll the ball five steps. There are several variables involved; therefore, you can not calibrate a putting stroke mechanically and ignore "feel."

In the previous section on posture, reference was made to the triangle created by the arms as a player prepares to make a putting stroke. In the square, or parallel and perpendicular approach, this triangular relationship is maintained as the arms move the putter away from the ball and the two arms working together return the putter down the imaginary target line through the ball toward the target. (Review Figure 3-5.) While it was mentioned that the elbows should not be held in a rigid position in order to maintain straight sides to the triangle, it is important that the "tip" of the triangle formed by the wrists, hands and putter shaft not be allowed to bend. *In both the putting stroke and the chipping stroke, which you will learn in Chapter 4, no wrist cocking or hinging are required as the wrists are held in the same position throughout the stroke.* The other two basic strokes permit, and even require, that the wrists be hinged (cocked and uncocked) during the swing.

As you will note from the previous paragraphs and illustrations, the putting stroke as presented in this manual is quite simple in that the number of variables have been reduced to an absolute minimum. There are, however, several admonitions that you will need to heed in order to maximize your success in the "putting game."

a. As the putter head is moved away from the ball, it is important to emphasize that the putter may be pushed with the left shoulder and arm or pulled with the right hand and arm.

b. Your ability to move the club away from the ball along an extension of the imaginary target line may be enhanced by a reverse overlapping grip that extends the forefinger of the left hand over the fingers of the right hand.

c. Keeping the putter blade perpendicular or "square" to the target line is critical to your success in rolling the ball toward your predetermined target.

d. As the putter head is moved away from the ball, it is important that the putter head is kept close to the putting surface.

e. Since it is important to maintain a straight left wrist in the putting stroke, a relatively slow "take away" is advisable.

f. After the putter head has been moved from the ball the distance you judge to be appropriate, it is important to move the putter head back through the ball with an accelerating pace. (See Figure 3-6.) *As with any of the four basic strokes, the club head should be accelerating through the ball and never be allowed to decelerate upon impact.*

g. There is no magic recipe for making the judgement about the distance that the putter head is taken away from the ball. There are many variables that influence this judgement or "feel." Some of those variables include the following: (1) the slope of the green over which the ball must travel, (2) the type and length of grass, and (3) the weight of the putter head itself. A considerable amount of experience with putting on the same greens will allow you to make better and more consistent judgments.

h. Since the putting stroke requires only arm movement, it is important for a player's head, torso and legs to remain as still as possible throughout the putting stroke. Both distance and direction are critical variables in putting which can be adversely affected by body movements during the putting stroke. *Try to see the club head strike the ball.*

i. It is suggested that players keep their eyes fixed on the ball during the putting stroke. On putts of five feet or less, which you can reasonable expect to make about 50% of the time, you should *listen for the ball to drop in the cup,* rather than *peek* during the stroke. The process of peeking will result in head movement that often causes the ball to be mis-hit.

j. On long putts of 30 feet or more, it is necessary for most players to allow the putter face to move inside the target line on the take away and back to the target line as the forward stroke is made. This movement of the club inside the target line on the back swing is necessitated because of the rotation of the upper body as the putter is pushed further away from the ball. This process of moving the putter inside the target line introduces a timing variable that may be particularly difficult for a beginner to accommodate. However, it should be acknowledged that some very successful players move the putter inside the target line on all putts regardless of their length.

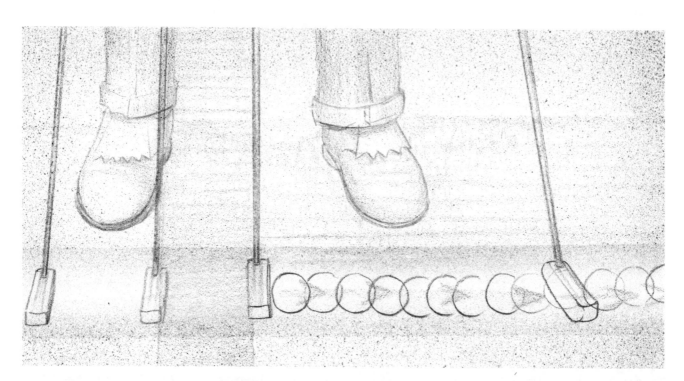

Fig. 3-6. Take Shorter Back Stroke Than Forward Stroke to Practice Acceleration of the Putter

The Golf Clinic
Poppy Hills Golf Course
Pebble Beach, CA

The Florida Golf School
Fort Pierce, FL

NOTES

NOTES

CHAPTER 4

THE CHIPPING STROKE

One of the strokes which is extremely important to the beginning or high handicap golfer is the chipping stroke. This stroke is used when the ball is relatively near the green (15-20 yards or closer), and the ball is bounced or rolled further than it will fly in the air. When the terrain between the ball and the cup is relatively flat (no mounds, bunkers or hazards), the ball can be stroked with a six iron in a manner that causes it to be airborne no more than about one-third of the distance between the position of the ball and the cup. The exact combination of the distance the ball travels in the air versus its roll after landing on the green is determined by several variables e.g., total distance to the cup, club selected, length of player's back swing, force exerted on forward swing, slope of putting surface, length and texture of grass. Nevertheless, the concept of one-third the distance in the air and two-thirds on the ground for a stroke around the green from a relatively flat area with a six iron is a good starting point. A considerable amount of practice is required for a player to develop a "feel" for the right combination of loft and roll distances necessary to stroke the ball to the cup in a consistent manner.

Grip. The basic grip as described and illustrated in Chapter 2 or as modified to the individual's preference for putting can be used for chipping. (See Figure 4-1.) In fact, greater control can be achieved by "choking down" or sliding the hands further down on the shaft. Some instructors suggest that separation of the hands by a distance of 1/2 inch to 1 inch will also increase control. Since this stroke does not require nearly as much physical strength or neuromuscular coordination as most other golf strokes, technique and practice can be expected to bring about improvement rapidly for the adult beginner. In other words, you can come closer to perfection with the chipping stroke and the putting strokes than with the other two basic strokes of golf.

Stance. The position of a player's body for this stroke is quite similar to the body position for the putting stroke. (See Chapter 3.) Since the objective is to minimize body movement, the player's feet need to be reasonably close together (6-12 inches apart). The player's relationship to the ball and the target line is the "square" to "slightly open" position. The toes of the right foot are on a line parallel to the target line and the ball is positioned perpendicular to the "toe line" and right of center on the target line. To avoid shifting of the body's center of gravity to the right during the stroke, it is necessary to have more of the body's mass supported by the left foot and leg than by the right. The hands are positioned "ahead" or to the left of the ball. If the ball is to be

Fig. 4-1   The Same Grip Used for Putting can be Used for Chipping

44

chipped on a low trajectory, it needs to be positioned right of center. (See Figure 4-2.)

The Short Low Chipping Stroke. The stroke is initiated by the left shoulder and arm pushing the club head away from the ball on the imaginary target line. If the distance from ball to cup (hole) requires that the club be pushed away or back from the ball more than 12 inches, the clubface will be moved in from the target line on the way back and returned to a square position upon impact. This movement of the clubface inside the target line on the longer stroke is necessary because of the body's natural rotation as the club moves further away from the ball. Any special effort to keep the clubface "square" or perpendicular to the line for more than 12-15 inches requires that the arms move further away from the body, thus causing a loss of control and consistency in the forward part of the stroke. As the left arm and shoulder push the club away from the ball on the imaginary target line, the left wrist remains firm as it neither bends up or down. The back of the left hand and the forearm are held in a straight although relaxed position. This straight and firm relationship of the left forearm and wrist increases consistency and solid contact of the clubface and the ball. The club head returns to the back of the ball on a slightly descending path as the club is pulled back to its original position by the left arm and shoulder. The right arm and shoulder are basically "along for the ride" except as the right hand helps to direct the clubface at the moment of contact.

The club chosen for this stroke when played from a location that is within a few yards of the green and level or uphill to the cup (hole) is typically the seven, six or five iron. The reason for these choices relates to the planned flight of the ball which is to have a low trajectory that allows the ball to bounce and roll two-thirds of the distance to the cup. The longer irons (1 through 4) have insufficient loft to get the ball airborne for approxi-

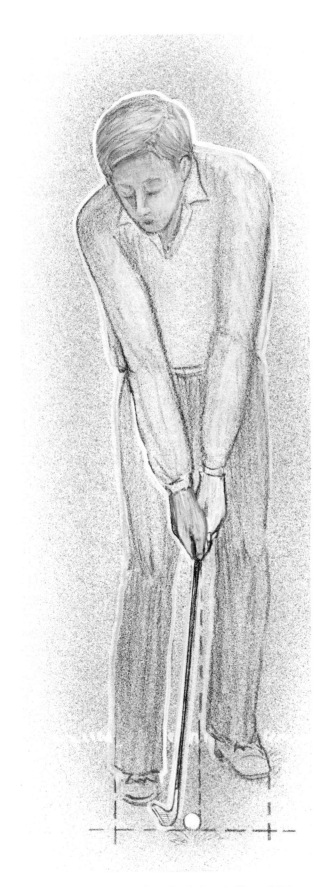

Fig. 4-2. Hands are Ahead of the Ball and More Weight is on the Left Foot When Chipping

45

mately one-third of the distance to the cup. (See Figure 4-3.) Also, their additional length and head weight make them difficult to control for this type of delicate stroke. Obviously long chip shots on large greens which may be 25 yards or more may be best made with the three or four iron. Short irons such as the wedge, 9 and 8 are not the best choice since they have too much loft to allow the necessary amount of roll.

Regardless of the club selected the ball is to be airborne for less distance than its bounce and roll. Also, the stroke must descend to the back of the ball. (See Figure 4-4.) *As with all golf strokes, the club must accelerate to and through the ball. There is no place in the game for a stroke that decelerates as the club approaches the ball.* The player must resist the "urge" to help or lift the ball with the club. The ball will move upward when a lofted club descends and contacts the ball near or below its equator. A proper chipping stroke strikes the turf immediately after the ball has been struck and becomes airborne. It is important to keep your body, including your head, very still during the stroke. If you try to see the shot too soon, it won't be worth the "peek."

The Longer and Higher Chipping Stroke. When the ball is located more than two or three yards from the green or when there is a mound, high grass or sand between you and the green, or when the green slopes downhill from you, a higher trajectory flight of the ball is required and correspondingly less roll after the ball lands on the putting surface. For this stroke a more lofted club such as the wedge or nine iron should be used although grip and posture are the same as for the short, low chipping stroke. However, because you are further from the green the stroke will be longer, i.e. the club will be pushed further away from the ball before the forward part of the stroke begins. As the club is pushed away from the ball, the club moves both inward and upward. The clubface moves from a position

Fig. 4-3. When the Green is Relatively Level, the Ball Should be Chipped on a Low Trajectory

Fig. 4-4. The Chip is a Descending Stroke

that is "square" or perpendicular to the target line to a position that is parallel to the target line with the toe of the club (the end of the clubface that is opposite the shaft) pointing upward. (See Figure 4-5.) As the club is pushed away and up from the ball, the club shaft moves to a position that is parallel to the target line and 3"-5" inside a player's toe line. Even a maximum chip of approximately 30 yards does not require the hands to be taken much higher than waist high. Throughout this stroke the left arm should remain firm in that there should be no noticeable bending or flexing of the elbow or wrist. This absence of wrist flexure or "break" is a distinguishing feature between the longer and higher chipping stroke and the pitching stroke as described in Chapter 5. Regardless of the length of the stroke, it is important to remember that the club must be accelerating to and "through" the ball. The descending and accelerating stroke plus the loft of the clubface will cause the ball to become airborne. (See Figure 4-6.) Resist any feelings that you need to help by lifting up during the stroke.

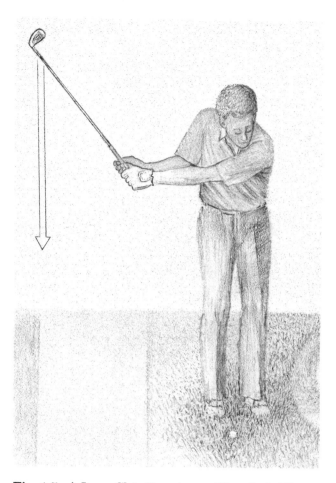

Fig. 4-5. A Long Chip Requires a Firm Left Elbow and Wrist

Strategy. After one understands the fundamentals of the chipping stroke, the mechanics can be learned in a relatively short period of time. The tactile ability required to stroke the ball with the right combination of direction and distance takes practice to develop "feel." Successful chipping also requires careful attention to the contour of the green, i. e. putting surface. For example, you will need to stroke the ball much harder if you have a relatively long uphill slope to negotiate. Conversely, the stroke required to carry the ball over an area of high grass to a downhill slope may require less force, a more lofted club and more flight time than roll. The slope of the green may require that you establish a target line several feet to the left or right of the cup as you plan the curving journey of the ball. There is no substitute for practice as one seeks to develop the psychomotor skill and the judge-

Fig. 4-6. Loft of the Club and Descending Stroke Gets Ball Airborne

47

ment necessary to achieve success with the chipping aspect of the game.

Remember the objective of the chipping stroke is to roll the ball into the cup or close enough so that only one putting stroke will be required. Just getting "on the green" is not enough.

NOTES

NOTES

CHAPTER 5

THE PITCHING STROKE

As one progresses from simple to complex in learning the four basic strokes of golf, more variables are introduced. For example, putting and chipping require a relatively short stroke that demands a minimum of body movement. In fact you were instructed to keep your body relatively still as your shoulder, upper chest, arm, wrist and hand move the club away from and back toward the ball. The pitching stroke is longer (the club moves a greater distance away from the ball), and as a result, the body turns away from the ball and turns back again as the forward part of the pitching stroke is made. Nevertheless, it is important for you to understand the relationship of the strokes since they have several common elements as well as some unique features.

The purpose of the pitching stroke is to cause the ball to become airborne for a distance of six to sixty yards and drop onto the green softly with minimal roll. The distance of six to sixty yards is only an approximation as it could be slightly more or less. The key factor in differentiating the pitching stroke from the chipping stroke is the hinging of the wrists which brings the shaft to near a 90 degree relationship with the left forearm at waist height. (See Figure 5-1.) This hinging action causes the ball to fly on a higher trajectory, to be airborne longer and land softly with minimal roll. Obviously the length of the stroke and the force needed to propel the ball six yards is

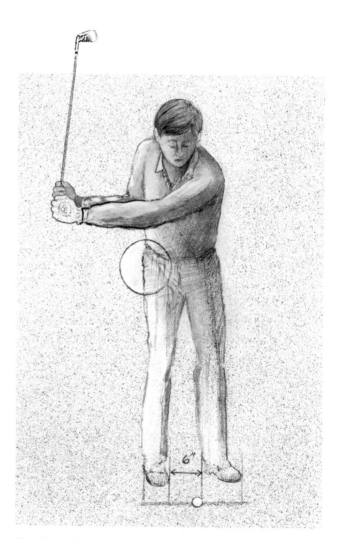

Fig. 5-1. Pitching Stroke Requires Wrist Cock

considerably less than that required to propel the ball sixty yards. This, of course, introduces several variables with which a player must deal, e.g. the distance the club moves away from the ball both horizontally

51

and vertically, the opening and closing of the face of the club in relation to the imaginary target line, the speed with which the club head moves toward and through the ball as well as the movement of the knees, waist, and shoulders in response to the length of the swing.

Grip. The basic grip as described and illustrated in Chapter 2 should be used when executing the pitching stroke. Remember to hold the club with light pressure. Gripping too tightly creates tension which inhibits the natural action of the club. Also, you can gain greater control by sliding your hands down on the shaft.

Stance. The static position of a player's body for pitching is as described and illustrated in Chapter 2. Because the pitching stroke is less than a full swing, and as a result, does not require full shoulder rotation or a major shift of body mass, your feet should be less than shoulder width apart. More of your weight will be on the left foot at address and for pitches of up to about 25 yards remain there throughout the pitching stroke. For pitch shots over 25 yards, you must shift some weight over to the inside of your right foot as the club goes up. This allows you to move your knees toward the target on the down swing. However, a beginning or high handicap player is advised to keep the pitching stroke simple with a relatively small amount of lower body movement. It is somewhat easier for the stroke to be made if the stance is opened. Opening the stance occurs as the left foot is pulled back several inches from a line parallel to the target line. (See Figure 5-2.)

The stroke. As with all of the basic strokes, the club head should be pushed away from the ball with the left shoulder, chest, and arm. After the club head is moved away from the ball a few inches it begins to also be raised upward by the pushing action of the left side of the chest, left shoulder and

Fig. 5-2. Opening the Stance Requires the Left Foot to be Pulled Back from the Target Line

52

arm. It is important that a player's left elbow remains relatively straight in order that the club is "pushed back" rather than "picked up" by the right hand. The natural rotation of the body will cause the club head to move in toward the player's toe line from the imaginary target line. As the club is pushed away from the ball and upward, the left wrist is cocked upward. (See Figure 5-3.)

The result of this series of movements can be verified as the club is observed at a position slightly above waist high. If the movement has been executed properly, the club shaft will be perpendicular to the left arm and above a point opposite the right foot with the shaft inclined slightly away from the target line as illustrated in Figure 5-2. In addition, there will be skin folds or slight wrinkles at the junction of the left hand and forearm. (This reveals the presence of the all important wrist cock.) From this intermediate position, the club is pushed upward the desired distance by the left side of the chest, left shoulder and arm.

The longer pitching stroke (25 yards or more) that requires lower body motion can be viewed as part of the *full swing* with an iron as described and illustrated in Chapters 6 and 7. It is important to emphasize that you need to develop a smooth set of motions as the arms are moved upward to approximately shoulder height on your right, then brought back and through the ball with the arms finishing about shoulder height on your left. (See Figure 5-4.)

The development of a smooth set of motions begins with your feet, ankles, and knees. Assume your standard stance as described and illustrated in Chapter 2. With your feet less than shoulder width apart, and without a club, begin to gently rock your weight from your left to your right and back again. Remember that a proper stance requires your knees to be bent forward; therefore, the left knee will swivel to the right as your weight moves to the inside of your right foot. As you turn back onto your left foot, the

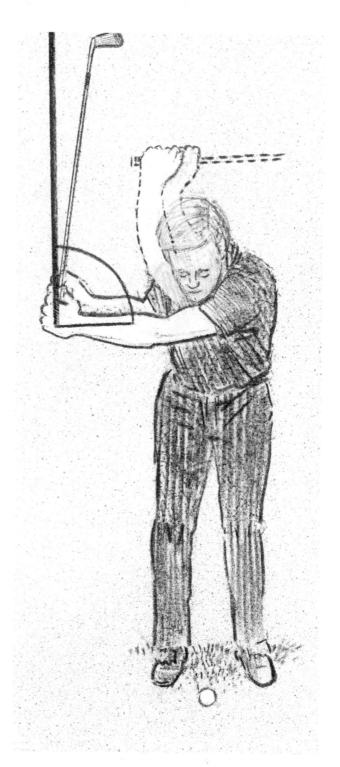

Fig. 5-3. The Left Wrist is Cocked Upward.

right knee will turn to the left. It is important to remember that the knees remain in a flexed position throughout this exercise. This is one of the most fundamental and critical set of motions in the game of golf. Unfortunately, some instructors overlook its importance since proficient golfers seem to make

Fig. 5-4. The Back Swing and Forward Swing are of Equal Length.

these motions "naturally." (See Figure 5-5.) Practice these motions since repetition is essential to build "neuromuscular consistency." As these motions are incorporated into the pitching stroke and later into the full swing, they will become integrated, and you will not have to think about the rocking motion.

After the movement of the feet, ankles, and knees are understood, repeat them sufficiently to create a smooth set of motions. Next, you need to understand and practice the movement of the wrists, forearms, upper arms, shoulders, and the muscles of the upper left side of the chest. With a proper grip and from a proper posture position as described and illustrated in Chapter 2 (no

golf ball yet), practice the movement of pushing the club away and upward. Your hands should be approximately waist high and the wrists should cock the club head upward in a 90 degree relationship with your forearm. This set of motions is also very critical to making the proper pitching stroke as well as the full swing later in your development. In the process of moving the club from a point on the ground directly in front of you to a point that is opposite your right side, the left forearm should rotate from a 90 degree relationship to the ground to approximately 70-75 degrees. (See Figure 5-6.) Forearm rotation is a very important concept that is too often assumed by instructors to occur "naturally." Now, without disturbing the wrist

Fig. 5-5. Flexed Knees With a Shift of Weight From
Left to Right and Back Again

Fig. 5-6. Forearm Rotation With Club Shaft in a 90
Degree Relationship.

55

and club relationship, pull and rotate the club with the left arm back toward its original position on the ground. As you approach the ground, both hands deliver the club head to and through the ball. (See Figure 5-7.) Your right hand and forearm follow the rotating left forearm as the club shaft is pulled through to the left side of your body. This combination of body rotation and clubface angle results in the desired trajectory. (See Figures 5-8a and 5-8b.)

The motions involved in moving the club from a position opposite your right side to a parallel position opposite your left side must be repeated many times to create neuromuscular consistency. These motions are essential to the execution of the golf swing in general and the pitching stroke in particular. The left elbow remains relatively straight throughout this set of body motions that rotates the arms as they move away from and back through their original position at address.

Fig. 5-7. Club is Pulled Back and Through the Ball

Craft-Zavichas Golf School
Tucson National Golf and
Conference Center
Tucson, AZ

Tucson National Golf and Conference Center
Tucson, AZ

Fig. 5-5.   Flexed Knees With a Shift of Weight From
Left to Right and Back Again

Fig. 5-6.   Forearm Rotation With Club Shaft in a 90
Degree Relationship.

and club relationship, pull and rotate the club with the left arm back toward its original position on the ground. As you approach the ground, both hands deliver the club head to and through the ball. (See Figure 5-7.) Your right hand and forearm follow the rotating left forearm as the club shaft is pulled through to the left side of your body. This combination of body rotation and clubface angle results in the desired trajectory. (See Figures 5-8a and 5-8b.)

The motions involved in moving the club from a position opposite your right side to a parallel position opposite your left side must be repeated many times to create neuromuscular consistency. These motions are essential to the execution of the golf swing in general and the pitching stroke in particular. The left elbow remains relatively straight throughout this set of body motions that rotates the arms as they move away from and back through their original position at address.

Fig. 5-7. Club is Pulled Back and Through the Ball

56

Fig. 5-8a-b. The Body's Rotation and the Clubface Angle Produce the Ball's Trajectory

NOTES

NOTES

CHAPTER 6

FULL SWING FUNDAMENTALS

This instruction manual describes the techniques involved in executing the four basic strokes inherent in the game of golf, i.e., putting, chipping, pitching, and the full swing with irons, fairway woods and the driver. The first three strokes involve a partial swing. Therefore, this chapter detailing the techniques of the full swing is placed at the midpoint in the sequence immediately preceding the three chapters that focus on strokes requiring a full swing.

My basic premise is that the principles and techniques involved in executing the full swing are the same whether the stroke is made with (1) a short iron, i.e., wedge, 9, 8, 7, (2) mid to long iron, i.e., 6, 5, 4, 3, (3) the fairway woods (7, 6, 5, 4, 3), or (4) the driver, i.e., number 1 and 2 woods or number 1 and 2 irons. The chapters that describe the full swing with irons, fairway woods and driver will provide information about the unique features of these strokes, variations in ball position, strategies for different conditions and the differences in the swing that are necessitated by or result from club head design and length of the club shaft. The longer the club, the further you should stand from the ball, the wider apart your feet should be, the more to the left the ball should be positioned in your stance and the more elliptical will be the shape of your swing. Therefore, while the driver approaches the ball on a slightly ascending angle, the short iron approaches the ball on a comparatively steep descending angle. (See Figures 6-1a to 6-1f.)

THE STATIC ELEMENTS OF THE SWING

The foundation for the four basic strokes of golf were described and illustrated in Chapter 2. The manner in which the hands hold the club, the alignment of the player's body to the ball and the target, as well as the player's posture, provide a foundation from which a golf stroke is taken. Whether the stroke involves a partial or full swing these foundation elements are essential. Because these elements occur before the club is placed in motion, some instructors refer to them collectively as the *static* part of the golf swing. Before attempting to develop the *dynamic* or motion part of the golf swing, it is important to review the fundamentals of the grip and stance which includes alignment and posture as described and illustrated in Chapter 2. Mastering these elements will lead to a consistent pre-swing routine.

THE DYNAMIC ELEMENTS OF THE SWING

The full swing builds upon other concepts you have learned and skills you have developed as you have progressed through Chapters 2, 3, 4 and 5. In fact, *the proper grip,*

Fig. 6-1a. Full Swing Mechanics are the Same with Both Woods and Irons.

Fig. 6-1b. Full Swing-9 iron

alignment and posture make it possible for you to execute the dynamic or motion part of the golf swing. It should be emphasized that visualization or mental pictures are important to psychomotor skill development. You will find that the figures which accompany the prose, or written descriptions, are essential as you picture or visualize the physical movements you must make to develop a consistent and effective golf swing. It is important for you to realize that the movements you are trying to execute are sometimes not being made as visualized and described. It is for this reason that you may need someone to observe your efforts to execute the dynamic elements of your swing. Observing yourself in a mirror at several points in the swing may also provide visual feedback as you verify your body position at various points in the swing process. Some of the more effective instructors will provide video tape feedback to indicate the swing elements that are being executed both correctly and incorrectly.

A key concept that you must accept and attempt to implement is that the hands and arms are *not* the major "players" in the full swing. The hands and arms are moved by centrifugal and rotating forces of the body. *Controlled body motion is essential to an effective and consistent golf swing.*

The Waggle. After you have established the foundation for your swing, it is time to "get moving." The "waggle" is more than a nervous movement of a golfer. Rather,

61

Fig. 6-1c Full Swing-5 iron

Fig. 6-1d Full Swing-5 iron

it is a purposeful motion. In fact, I like to emphasize two purposes. First, the moving of the club head a foot or two away from the ball helps to begin the body's transition from the *static* to the *dynamic* or moving part of the swing. Even though this *PRIMER* and other instructional materials provide tedious details regarding the various elements of the golf swing, it is extremely important that you avoid rigid or jerky body movements. You may remember the principles of inertia from a previous science course. *A body at rest tends to remain at rest; a body in motion tends to remain in motion.* Second, the waggle begins to *cue* the body's central nerve center for the movements that are to follow. (See Figure 6-2.) These cues can relate to the path of the take away, the role of the legs, shoulder, forearm, wrist or other swing thoughts.

The Forward Press. An effective swing requires a shifting of some of your body's mass from left leg to right leg and back again. The forward press can help get you moving. It can also shift a bit of the body mass to the left so the "take away" can have some body mass to move to the right. For a beginner, the forward press is optional and not the most important move to make; however, it can help in the development of a smooth and coordinated series of movements. As illustrated the forward press does not require exaggerated movements. (See Figure 6-3.) In fact, the motion is almost imperceptible to others. The forward press involves a shift of body mass (weight) from an

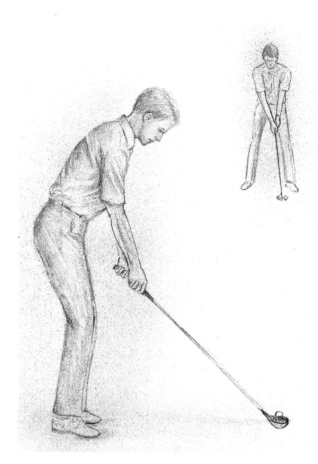

Fig. 6-1e Full Swing-driver

Fig. 6-2. The Waggle is a Purposeful Movement That Initiates the Dynamic Part of the Swing.

even distribution on both legs to perhaps as little as 10 percent more onto the left leg as the right knee moves an inch or two toward the left. Simultaneously there is movement of the left arm and club shaft an inch or so forward to position them on a line slightly in front of the club head and ball.

The take away and turn. While the foundation for the swing is set by your grip, alignment, and posture (Review Chapter 2), the manner in which the club is moved back or away from the ball determines, in large measure, the club's position at the top of the

Fig. 6-1f Full Swing-driver

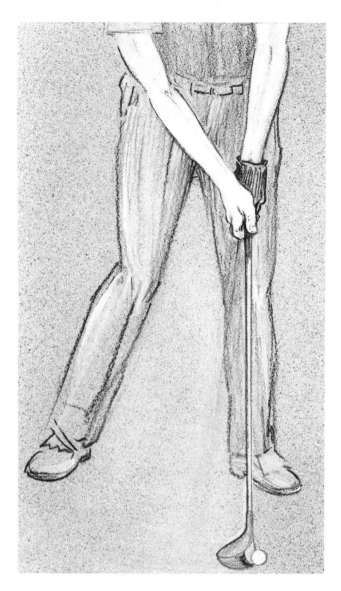

Fig. 6-3. The Forward Press Shifts a Bit of Weight to the Left Before Starting the Takeaway.

swing and the path on which the club head travels as it is brought back to the ball. Even though there are some differences in the "take away" motion as a result of the type and length of club which will be explained in greater detail in Chapters 7, 8, and 9, the key elements of the take away remain the same.

The waist and upper body, the left shoulder, the muscles of the upper left chest and a firm left arm control the "take away" which could be more properly called the *turn away*. Even though *the club head is pushed straight back from the ball on an extension of the imaginary target line for about six to twelve inches, the natural turning of the*

waist causes the club head to move inside the extension of the target line. (See Figure 6-4.) As the club head is pushed back, or away from the ball, the left shoulder and upper side of the left chest rotate to their eventual destination. You should be able to look over the point of your left shoulder and see the ball. The left knee rotates inward and the left forearm rolls naturally as the club is pushed back. This combination of pushing and rotation motion should move the club head to your first *checkpoint*. At a point between knee high and waist high, with the left arm touching your chest and fully extended on an imaginary line parallel to the target line which would run through your feet, the rotation of the left forearm has caused the toe of the clubface to point upward. (See Figure 6-5.)

The natural rotation of the waist and upper body in response to the *take away* begins the part of the swing referred to as the "turn." In reality the arms and club move in an arc around the spine which is the "hub" of your swing. Understanding the turn is of vital importance to the generation of power and the achievement of consistency. In this turning process body weight shifts from the left leg to the right leg. In fact, the flexed left knee bends forward and right as it points slightly behind the ball. The left heel will rise slightly in response to the body's turn or coil to the right. You should feel that the inside of the right leg and foot become an anchor for your swing. A note of caution is appropriate as you must not allow the *turn away* to cause your upper body to shift so far to the right that your right leg becomes perpendicular to the ground, or even worse, become inclined to the right beyond perpendicular. The right leg must maintain the inclined position of approximately 75-80 degrees for the swing to be made effectively. (See Figure 6-6.)

After the first checkpoint when you verify that the location of the club in relationship to the target line, you continue your turn and the left wrist begins the cocking

Fig. 6-4. Initiating the Takeaway

Fig. 6-5. The First Checkpoint to Determine the
Position of the Club and the Left Forearm

action as the shaft is brought into a 90 degree or perpendicular relationship with your extended left arm (not perpendicular to the ground). The forearm rotation causes the club shaft to be at an angle of about 70-75 degrees with the ground, although the shaft is at approximately 90 degrees with the rotated forearm. (See Figure 6-7.) The second checkpoint occurs as the left arm is above waist high. You can now verify that (1) the arm is above that imaginary line running through your feet and parallel to the target line, (2) your left elbow is relatively straight (not rigid and tense), (3) the left wrist is cocked upward (not bent left or right), and (4) the shaft is perpendicular to the left arm. (See Figures 6- 8 and 6 - 9.) This position creates the leverage needed in order to stroke the ball for both distance and direction.

Finishing the turn (coil). After verifying the position of the club and body position at the second check point, the turning or coiling continues. The muscles of the left side of the chest, the left shoulder, and arm keep pushing the club upward on an imaginary inclined line or more accurately, an imaginary plane. As illustrated in Figure 6-9, this plane extends from the ball through your upper body emerging behind your shoulder region. The angle of this imaginary plane varies with the player's height, i.e., the taller the player, the steeper the plane on which the club moves.

The swing angle is set or determined by the player's take away. The turn of your body brings the club inside the imaginary target line. The rotation of the left forearm sets the angle of the club shaft to the ground.

Fig. 6-6. The Angular Relationship of the Right Leg

This becomes the angle of the plane on which the club shaft is pushed upward as you finish the turn. At the second check point you were advised to observe the wrist cock. (Notice the slight wrinkles formed at the junction of the left forearm and thumb as the thumb points in the direction of the inside of your elbow.) The club shaft is positioned at ap- proximately 90 degrees with the forearm. The club shaft and the forearm are inclined away from the target line and form the inclined plane for the remainder of the swing. This left arm and club shaft relationship is maintained as the backswing is completed. The turning of the upper body and waist in response to the pushing of the left shoulder

Fig. 6-7. The Second Checkpoint Verifies That the Left Arm is Extended and Left Wrist Cocked.

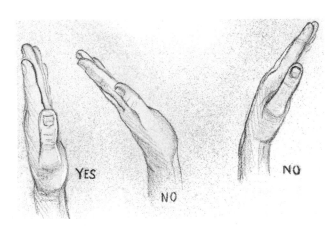

Fig. 6-8. Proper Position of the Left Wrist

Fig. 6-9. The Relationship of Left Arm and Club Shaft and the Path or Plane on Which the Club Moves

and the muscles of the upper left side of the chest creates a substantial amount of potential energy that is released when the club is returned to and through the ball. (See Figure 6-10.)

The turn is finished as the left shoulder rotates to a position from which you can look directly down at the ball. It is important to emphasize that the tilt of the shoulders enable the shoulder to move under and not push the chin aside. Likewise, the chin must be held away from the top of the chest as the stance is made, in order to allow the proper shoulder rotation. A thick body type or limited flexibility may preclude a full shoulder rotation, but as a beginner, you are urged to do the best that you can to increase flexibility and increase the coiling action.

During the turn the left arm moves up the plane established at the waist-high level which was the second check point. The left elbow is kept relatively firm although not rigid. The right elbow folds and remains relatively close to the body and points downward. (Review Figure 6-9.) This is an important point to remember since a "flying" right elbow can create several problems as the *downswing* is made. Also note that the 90 degree relationship between the left arm and the club shaft that was created when the turn began and the left wrist was "cocked", is maintained as the rotation of the shoulders is completed. This shoulder rotation should bring the hands to approximately the height of your head and the shaft of the club will be closer to a horizontal than vertical position. It must be emphasized that an individual's body type and flexibility will determine the extent to which the club shaft reaches the "ideal" or horizontal position achieved by some prominent professional players. Perhaps this is a good place to insert the admonition that *"the ball is not struck with the backswing." The implication is that you make a smooth, rhythmic backswing, not fast, as you slowly coil to the top of the backswing.*

Fig. 6-10. The Turn of the Waist and the Left Shoulder Move the Club to the Top

The top of the backswing. The ideal turn, or coil that results in a (1) firm and relatively straight left arm, (2) the left shoulder opposite the chin, and (3) the shaft of the club more horizontal than vertical is seldom achieved by most amateur golfers, not to mention some very successful professional golfers. (Review Figure 6-10.) Therefore, a beginner or high handicap player does not need to despair. Compromises with these three important elements can be and are made without causing disastrous results. In fact, the downswing success can be quite good and quite consistent even though the "ideal" position is not achieved at the top of the swing. (See Figure 6-11a.)

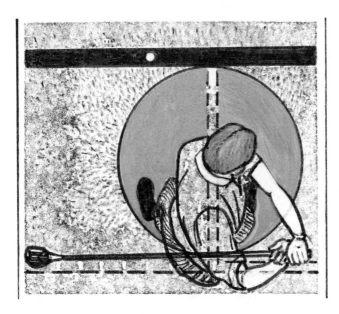

Fig. 6-11a. The Third Checkpoint is at the Top of the Back Swing

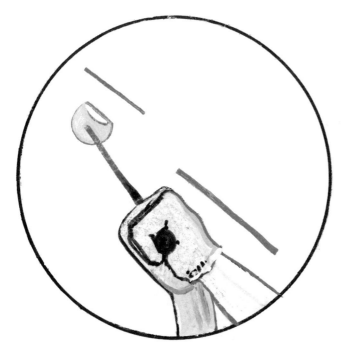

Fig. 6-11b. The Clubface Position at the Top

The third and final check point of the full swing is *at the top*. In addition to the three important elements previously mentioned, the following points must be checked by an observer, use of a full length mirror or through the use of a video tape recorder.

1. The shaft of the club should be parallel to your target line and more horizontal than vertical.
2. The face of the club should have the same incline as the plane or path on which the arms moved to the top. (See Figure 6-11b.)
3. The back of the left hand and the left forearm should be in alignment. There should be no inward or outward bending of the wrist. (Review Figures 6-11 and 6-8.)
4. The left arm should be firm and relatively extended, although not rigid. The position specified here and in Number 1 above can be achieved only by increasing your flexibility.
5. The wrist cock that was established someplace between the waist high and shoulder high positions of the left arm should be maintained. The juncture of the thumb and wrist is hinged or cocked in the direction of the inside of the elbow.
6. The right elbow should point more downward than outward (more vertical than horizontal), and the palm of the left hand faces downward while the palm of the right hand faces upward. (See Figure 6-12.)
7. The point of the left shoulder should be visible as you look down at the ball.
8. The rotation of the upper body should result in your belt buckle facing away from the target and your back toward the target. (See Figure 6-13.)

Fig. 6-12. The Left Arm, Wrist and Clubface Remain
in Alignment; Right Elbow Points Down

Fig. 6-13. Waist Rotation Back and Forward

9. The rotation occurs with a relatively small amount of lateral movement to the right. In fact, it is important that the right leg be slightly inclined approximately 10 degrees from perpendicular (90) toward the target. The coiling occurs with pressure along the inside of the right leg down to the inside of the right foot. (Review Figure 6-13.)

10. The knees should remain flexed. The left knee should point slightly behind the ball. The left heel will have raised an inch or so above the ground as the turn is completed. (Review Figure 6-13.)

Individuals having difficulty establishing the positions described in numbers 9 and 10 above should consider the device endorsed by professional Johnny Miller, called the *Turnmaster*. As mentioned previously, the correct positions at the top of the swing are determined, in large part, by the correct posture and the take away. Obviously, the swing occurs too rapidly to "think" yourself through the action. In fact, you should avoid any conscious use of the hands and arms during the swing. The check points are to help you analyze the body and club positions as you continue the skill building process. In other words, if the body and the club are not in the correct positions at certain points in the swing, the balance of the swing will be adversely affected. These positions and checkpoints are for learning and practice. When you execute the dynamic part of the swing, you must limit yourself to one or two thoughts, or you will suffer "paralysis through analysis".

70

Fig. 6-16. Rotation of the Waist Accelerates the Clubhead

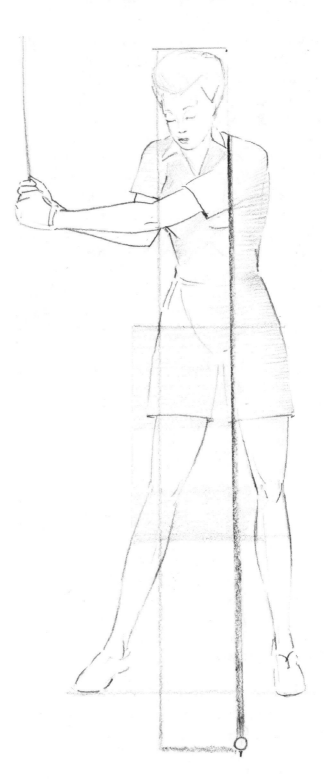

Fig. 6-17. Shift of Lower Body to the Left Leg is Essential to an Effective Swing; Maintain the Wrist Cock on the Way Back to the Ball

This becomes the moment of truth when all of the static and dynamic elements of the swing pave the way and determine in large measure the way in which the face of the club contacts the ball and the resulting flight of the ball. (See Ball Flight Laws and Figure 0-4.)

Lower body movement is the key. If you have the correct position at the top and move your lower body to the left, the swing takes care of itself. The left shoulder and arm continue the pulling action with the left wrist remaining in a "cocked" position until the hands approach waist height when both arms and hands accelerate the head of the club through the ball. (See Figure 6-17.) The accelerating rotary motion is vital to a successful swing. If you become too "ball-oriented" there is a tendency for the right arm and hand to begin a hitting action much too early in the swing. Also there is a tendency to slow the swing at impact. It may be helpful to focus on the swing and see the ball as something that just happens to be in the path of the club. Although you may not actually see the impact of the club and the ball, you should try to see the impact. This focus helps to keep your head and left shoulder from raising up before impact. Raising the head and/or left shoulder before impact often results in a "topped" shot or a "fat" shot as the right hand slams the club downward in response to the lifting action of the head and/or left shoulder.

The length of the path or arc on which the club head travels, the speed of the club head and position of the club head at impact determine, in large part, the length of the shot made with a given club.

POST-IMPACT SWING ELEMENTS

After impact, which has both arms extended, the left elbow folds and the left wrist recocks to bring the club head back up. The club head points toward the target on its way up and over as the hands end up in a position near your left ear. (See Figure 6-18.) The shifting of your lower body to the left and the body's rotation causes (1) your belt buckle to be facing the general direction of your target, (2) your weight to be on your left foot, and (3) your right heel to be off the ground. Gary Player in his book, *Golf After 50* suggests that you allow the right foot to move forward in a stepping motion to reduce the pressure on your back muscles.

Feeling The Swing

This chapter gave you an opportunity to understand the mechanics of the golf swing. Understanding is important to learning. However, neuromuscular skill requires much more than knowledge and

Fig. 6-18.   After Impact the Clubhead Moves Out to the Target and Upward to a Finish

understanding. You also need visual images and correct body movement. This is where the right hemisphere plays a major role in learning and executing the golf swing. You must develop a "feel" for the correct swing. Do not allow yourself to be "bogged" down with the mechanics during the swing. Do not attempt to practice a slow full swing. Practice the full swing at or near full speed. Slow motion is only for understanding the mechanics of the swing and checking on club and body position. The swing must be free, full, accelerating and uninterrupted once you have "paused" at the top.

74

NOTES

NOTES

CHAPTER 7

STROKING WITH IRONS

As pointed out at the beginning of Chapter 6, the elements involved with the full swing are the same with all clubs. However, the length of the club, the loft or angle of the clubface, and the position of the ball influence the execution of the swing elements.

As a beginner, you will be able to achieve a higher level of success with the short irons, in part, because of the shorter shaft of the club and the loft of the clubface. However, part of the reason for the higher level of success with the shorter clubs results from the fact that the dynamic elements of the swing do not have to be executed with as much precision as with the longer clubs to produce comparable results. You will note that the author has deliberately not included the long irons (3, 2, 1) in this chapter because they are difficult for a beginner and high handicap golfer to use effectively. After you have learned to apply the full-swing techniques to the short and middle irons, you can then begin to practice and apply full-swing techniques to the long irons.

As you practice the full swing with irons, it is essential that you review the static elements described and illustrated in Chapter 2. You cannot build an effective and consistent golf swing without a solid foundation composed of a proper grip, align-

ment and posture. For example, a poor grip that allows the clubface to be in a position other than perpendicular to the target line at impact will result in an unsatisfactory shot regardless of the proper execution of the swing elements. Likewise, faulty body alignment can make it impossible for you to execute the swing elements correctly. As a result, the club head cannot be returned to the ball in a manner that will produce a successful shot.

As an aid to help in the verification of your alignment, you can lay a club on the ground with the shaft parallel to your toes. Then by walking around and sighting down the club shaft, you can determine if your feet were parallel to the target line. If the club shaft is not parallel, move it to a parallel alignment with the target line and return to your position. Since your shoulders and hips also must be parallel to this line, you may need the help of someone else to assist you during your practice sessions.

In addition to your grip and your alignment, the maintenance of a proper body posture must be a part of each practice session. The angular relationship of your body, head, arms, thighs, and lower legs allow the dynamic elements of the swing to be made correctly. Even though you can observe and correct your posture in a full length mirror, you may need someone to observe your posture when practicing the full swing. (See Figures 7-1a-1d.)

As you practice and become more consistent with the iron stroke you will need to estimate the distance you can expect to carry and roll the ball with the different clubs. There is no standard that you "should" achieve. Your size, strength, body type and condition will determine your upper limits. Golf courses have yardage markers that help you to estimate distance to the green; therefore, you need to know the approximate yardage you can expect to carry and roll the ball with each club. Since the iron stroke is usually used to carry the ball to the green, knowing the distance is important. For example, if your 6 iron carries the ball 110 yards, you have a guide to the distances you can expect from your other irons. You can expect approximately 8-10 yards more for each smaller number club, e.g. 6, 5, 4 or less for each higher number e.g. 6, 7, 8, and 9.

THE SHORT IRON STROKE (7, 8, 9 and Wedges)

Application of the full swing elements to the 7, 8, and 9 irons and wedges is somewhat easier for the typical beginner. There-

Fig. 7-1a-d. Review of Alignment and Posture Fundamentals

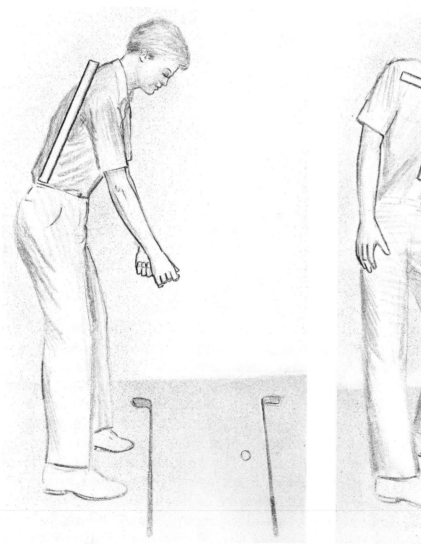

Fig. 7-1a

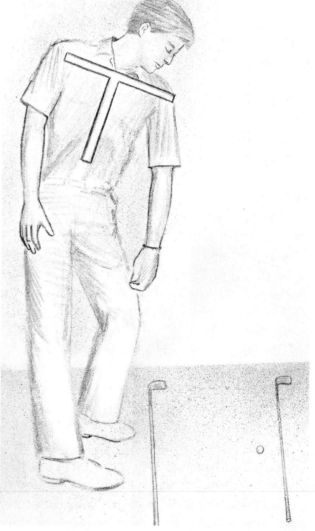

Fig. 7-1b

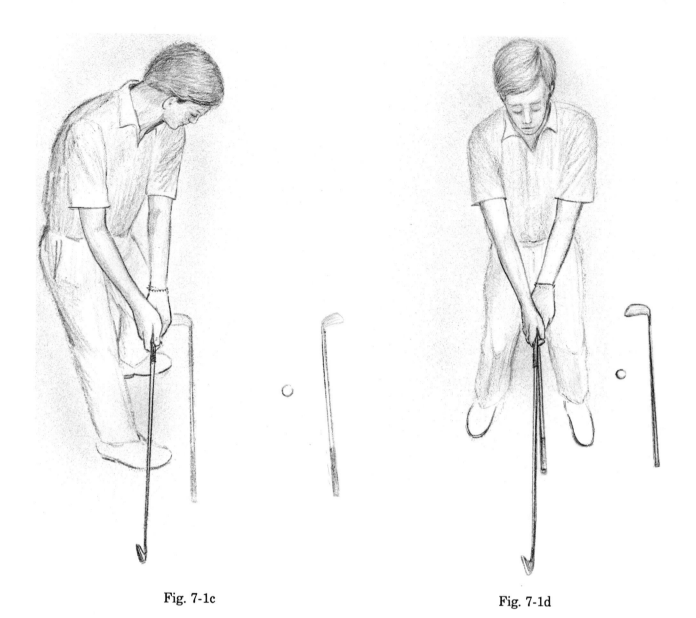

Fig. 7-1c   Fig. 7-1d

fore, you are encouraged to execute the full swing elements with these clubs before progressing on with other irons and woods. The shorter shaft enables you to control the path of the club away from and back through the ball. In addition, the greater degree of loft in the clubface allows you to get the ball airborne more consistently. Conversely, the longer irons and the woods are typically more difficult to control and the lesser degree of loft results in a lower trajectory and less consistent results.

     Even though the full swing elements are the same for all clubs, the length of the club and loft of the clubface requires a couple of modifications. First, these clubs are designed to help you send the ball on a relatively high trajectory for the purpose of landing on the green with only a relatively small amount of roll. (See Figure 7-2.) To accomplish this purpose, the clubface must contact the lower half of the ball on a rather steep angle of descent. The shorter shaft causes the club to be taken up on a relatively steep arc as the firm left arm pushes the club upward and the left shoulder rotates on a path below the chin. The club follows a similar arc coming back to and through the ball. A properly executed stroke with the short iron brings the club head into contact

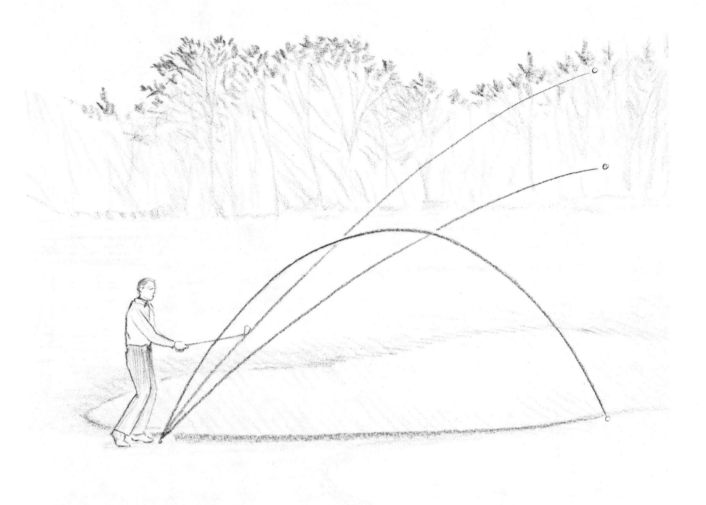

Fig. 7-2. Trajectory of Ball Flight Stroked with Short Irons

with the lower half of the back of the ball. As the club continues its descent through the ball, the ball rebounds upward and outward and the leading edge of the club slices through the turf slightly in front of the original location of the ball. (See Figure 7-3.) The piece of turf dislodged in this manner is referred to as a "divot."

A second modification required by the length of the club is the location of the ball on the target line in relation to the center of your body. As a general rule, the shorter the club, the closer the ball will be to your toe line. A good rule of thumb to follow is to play the 5, 6 and 7 iron slightly to the left of the mid point between your feet. Then locate the ball at the mid point or an inch or so further right for the shorter clubs, i.e. 8, 9 and wedges. (See Figure 7-4.) The longer clubs, 4, 3, and 2 would be located an inch or so more to the left. This general rule is not an absolute. Some instructors prefer to have the ball positioned at the same point on the ground in relationship to the center of the body. However, because the feet are closer together for shorter clubs, the ball is progressively closer to a line perpendicular to the instep of the right foot. Conversely, the

80

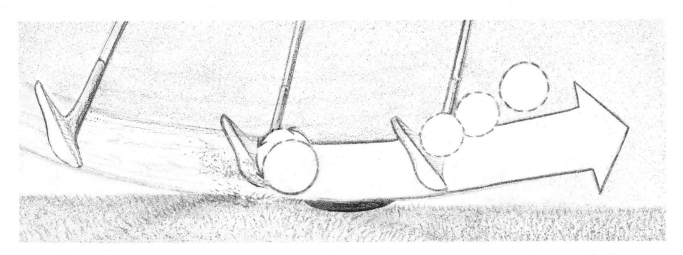

Fig. 7-3. A Steep Arc that Returns Through the Bottom One-Third of the Ball Takes a Proper Divot

ball is located further away from the right foot as longer clubs are used. The location of the ball may need to be modified for you under the direction of a professional instructor since the amount of lower body shift to the left as you initiate the downswing will determine in large part, the optimum position for the ball as the stroke is made with the differing club lengths. A good guideline to follow for the full swing is to play the ball as far toward the left foot as your lower body shift will allow.

With the preceding two modifications in mind, the full-swing techniques described and illustrated in Chapter 6 can be employed to develop a consistent and effective short iron stroke. The more lofted the clubface or the smaller the angle between the back of the clubface and the ground, the higher the trajectory of the shot and the shorter the distance the ball will carry in the air. Therefore, the distance the ball is from the green will be the primary factor in selecting the club to be used for a given golf shot. As you learn to execute the iron stroke correctly and consistently, you will find it essential to measure the number of yards that a ball will carry as you use different clubs. For example, a full swing with the 9 iron will cause the flight of the ball to be further than a full swing with the pitching wedge. Likewise, a full swing with the 7 iron will cause the ball to carry further than a full swing with an 8 iron.

Players differ because of numerous factors in terms of the distance that they can hit a golf ball with a given club as well as the difference in the distance that a ball will carry as a result of using clubs with different degrees of loft. However, the basic principle to remember is that the higher the number of the club, the higher the ball's trajectory will be and the shorter the distance the ball will travel in the air. Likewise, the higher the ball's trajectory, the more limited will be the amount of roll after the ball hits the ground.

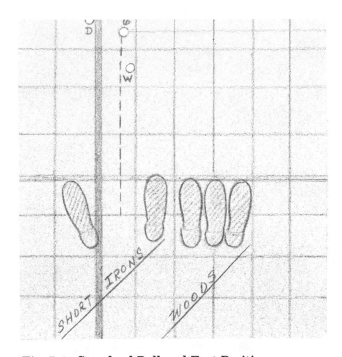

Fig. 7-4. Standard Ball and Foot Position

THE MIDDLE IRON STROKE (4, 5, 6)

The transition from the short irons to middle irons is relatively easy. The distinguishing features are a slightly longer shaft and a little less loft in the face of each smaller numbered iron. It may help you to realize that there is less difference between the short iron (7) and the middle iron (6) than between the 7 and 9 short irons. Although the difference in the length of the shaft and the loft from one number to the next is relatively small and hardly noticeable, the same swing with a 6 iron may carry the ball 10 to 15 yards further than with a 7 iron. Because of the longer shaft it will take you a slightly longer time to execute the full swing with a 5 iron than with a 9 iron. The ball position for the middle iron stroke needs to be on the imaginary target line and a bit more to the left of a point perpendicular to the middle of your body than may be the case with the short iron stroke. This difference is due, in part, to the fact that a middle iron has a longer shaft than a short iron, and the slope of the clubface is less lofted than the face of the shorter irons. The only other point of emphasis needed is that the pause at the top of your backswing needs to be a bit more pronounced for longer clubs as the longer shaft is pulled back on the plane toward the ball and the knees and lower body shift to the left on a line parallel to the target.

The difficulty some beginners have with the longer irons is the fact that they try to jerk the longer irons back and forth rapidly. As a result, the lower body does not have time to make the necessary shift to the left. As a meaningful generalization, the longer the club, the slower the takeaway and coil and the more deliberate the pause needs to be before the downswing begins. Remember, you do not strike the ball with the back swing. It is the distance the club head travels back to the ball and its speed that determines the force exerted on the ball at impact.

As described for the short iron, the middle iron requires a descending path through the ball. As the right arm rolls toward the left, the club head is recocked as the arms take it to a high finish. (See Figure 7-5.) The loft of the club helps to get the ball airborne; therefore, you need to avoid any lifting or sweeping action.

THE LONG IRON STROKE (1, 2, 3)

As indicated in the introduction to this chapter, it is my judgment that beginners or high handicap players should not utilize the long irons unless and until they have developed the full swing techniques to the point where the swing can be executed consistently and successfully with the middle irons. In fact, most experienced amateur golfers whose handicaps are 20 or higher would be well advised to consider using lofted, fairway woods such as the 8, 7, or 6, instead of the long irons from the fairway. However, the use of long irons for the tee shot may be an option to be considered by beginners and high handicapped golfers. This will be discussed further in Chapter 9.

TROUBLE SHOTS

The descriptions and illustrations for the golf swing assume a relatively flat location on the fairway or the teeing area. Obviously, when the ball is located on a sloping surface, in the rough with longer grass, within a grove of trees with overhanging limbs or in a sand bunker, modifications must be made in the basic swing techniques in order to execute the stroke effectively. While these shots are frequently referred to as "trouble shots", they will be much less trouble to you if you understand the modifications that must be made in the position of the ball in your stance and your body alignment. Body balance is critical in the execution of these shots. Often you may have to take less than a full swing in order to maintain your balance.

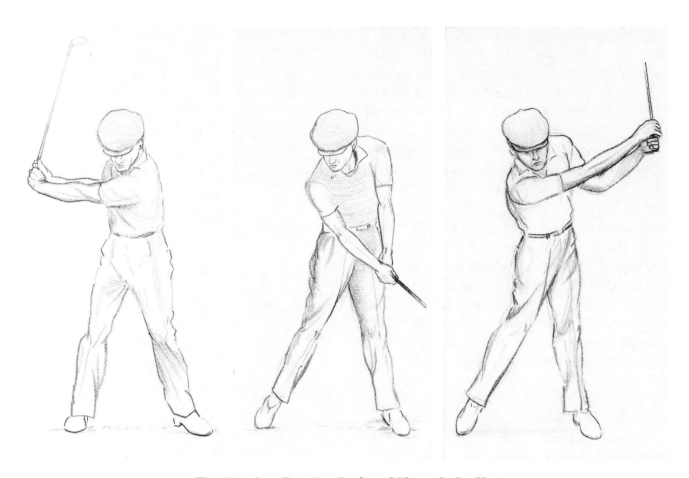

Fig. 7-5. Arm Rotation Back and Through the Shot

Sidehill lie: ball above your feet.
With a sidehill lie where the ball is above your feet, it is necessary to move your hands down on the shaft (choke down) since the slope of the ground actually brings the ball closer to your hands. A practice swing or two along the slope will allow you to gauge the amount that you should slide your hands down the shaft. A second modification that must be made is that the ball must be located more toward the right foot than normal in order to avoid pulling or "hooking" the ball to the left. No other modifications should be necessary to execute this shot successfully. It is important that the grip and your posture not be altered. (See Figure 7-6.)

Sidehill lie: ball below your feet.
In this position, the ball is further away from your hands; therefore, you will need to bend your knees a bit more than usual,

Fig. 7-6. Choke down on Grip when Ball is Above Your Feet; Expect the Ball to Bend Left.

83

widen your stance, and shift your weight more toward your heels to counteract the pull of gravity as you execute the stroke. When a shot is made from this type of lie, the ball will normally curve to the right or *downhill*. Therefore, it is necessary to align your body and establish a target line to the left of the intended landing area. Although no additional modification need be made for a stroke from this location, you will have to make an extra effort to push the club back from the ball and into a position opposite your right foot as the club goes upward. The reason that this motion takes extra concentration from this type of lie is the fact that you are moving the club against the pull of gravity as you move the club back inside to a position opposite the right leg. (See Figure 7-7.)

Uphill lie. When the ball rests on a slope that extends upward toward the intended target, several modifications must be made in order to execute the shot effectively. If a full swing is to be executed from this type of uphill lie, you will need to exercise considerable caution to avoid a shift of the body's mass down the slope as the club is taken away from the ball and upward. If you are close to the green and are only taking a partial stroke, the pull of gravity will be less of a problem. In any type of stroke from this type of lie you need to align your shoulders parallel to the slope of the ground, and the ball location on the target line should be a bit more toward the uphill foot. With a partial stroke, you are advised to keep as much of your weight as possible on the inside of your right foot. (See Figure 7-8.) Because of the ball's location on the upward slope, the ball will fly on a higher trajectory when struck solidly; therefore, you may want to use a less lofted club. For example, you may achieve the same trajectory from an uphill lie with a 7 iron as you would with a 9 iron from a regular lie.

Fig. 7-7. Hold Grip at End; Keep Knees Flexed Through the Swing; Expect Ball to Bend Right

Downhill lie. When the ball is located on a downward slope toward the target, it is necessary to play the ball back in your stance or more nearly perpendicular to the right foot than would be the case with a normal lie. As with the uphill lie, you need to align the shoulders parallel to the slope and take one or two practice swings to locate the exact point at which the club head will be at the lowest position on the arc of the swing. (See Figure 7-9.) When the ball is positioned back in the stance or more nearly perpendicular to the right foot, the swing will cause the trajectory of the ball to be lower than when the ball is played toward the midpoint of the stance from a level lie. For example, it may be necessary for you to use a 9 iron in order to achieve the trajectory that you would normally achieve with a 6 iron from a flat or level lie.

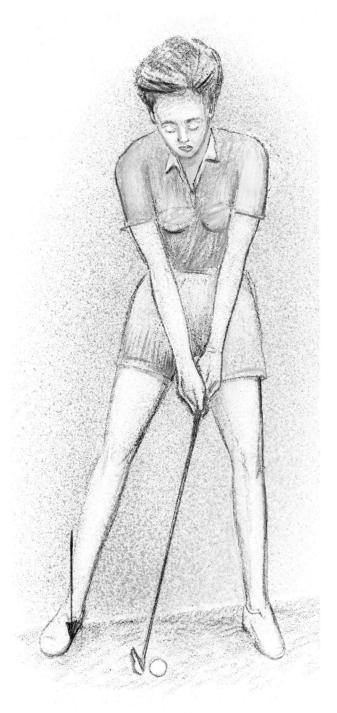

Fig. 7-8. Align Shoulders With Slope and Use Less
Lofted Club

Fig. 7-9. Align Shoulders With Slope and Position
Ball Perpendicular to Right Foot.

85

Ball located in a grove of trees or under overhanging limbs. When the ball is located within a grove of trees or under overhanging branches, it is usually best to chip the ball on a low trajectory through an opening on the safest line to return the ball to the fairway. (See Figure 7-10.) The choice of club to use in this situation depends on the height of any overhanging limbs. The key to this shot is to play the ball back in the stance or on a line nearly perpendicular to the right foot with the club shaft inclined forward and the hands somewhat near the midpoint of your stance. (See Figure 7-11.) The club is pushed back to a position between knee high and waist high with little or no cocking of the left wrist. This shot is executed much like the chipping stroke although most golfers refer to this as a "punch" shot. By keeping the left elbow and wrist in a somewhat fixed position and the weight more on the left than the right, there is very little transfer of weight for this stroke as the club is pushed away and brought back to the ball with the left shoulder and arm.

Fig. 7-10. Play the Safest Route to the Fairway.

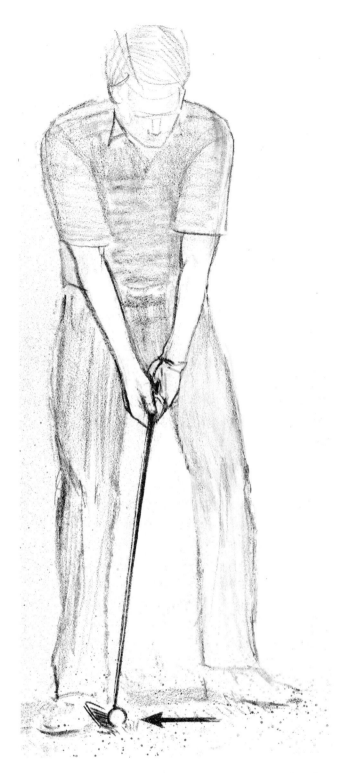

Fig. 7-11.   Position Ball More Nearly Perpendicular to Right Foot and Chip Ball with Little or No Wrist Cock.

Bunker shots. Execution of shots from fairway or green-side bunkers or "traps" require a considerable amount of practice as well as careful attention to proper tech-

Fig. 7-12.   Feet Must be Firm to Avoid Body Movement as Stroke is Made

nique. A shot made from a fairway sand bunker is executed like any other full iron shot if (1) the ball is setting up on the surface of the sand, and (2) the bunker is not too deep (sides that are not more than a foot or two higher than the surface of the bunker). The most important thing to remember is that you must have a firm foundation which may require you to twist your feet a bit to make sure you can execute a full or nearly full swing without your feet slipping in the sand. (See Figure 7-12.) By working your feet into the sand about an inch below the surface, you will have lowered yourself in relation to the ball. Therefore, it is important to slide your hands an inch or so downward on the shaft to avoid hitting behind the ball when you take a full swing. To maintain balance from a fairway sand bunker, you must reduce the amount of weight transfer and lower-body movement. This will reduce your power; therefore, you will need a lower numbered club for a given distance than you would from a regular fairway lie. (See Figure 7-13.) This somewhat restricted swing

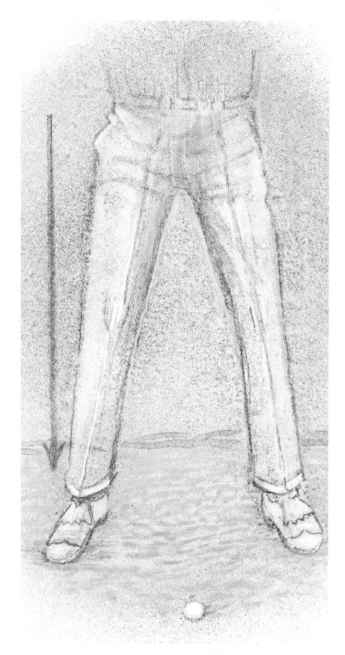

Fig. 7-13. Less Than a Full Swing Will Avoid Slipping of Feet in Sand

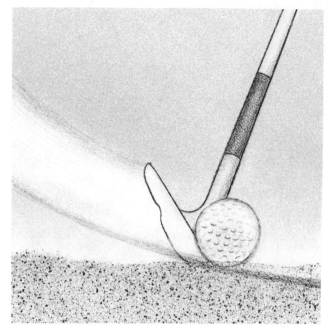

Fig. 7-14. Strike the Ball Before Sand for Maximum Distance

"exploded" out of the sand and onto the fairway. (See Figure 7-15.) Add a sand wedge to your set. Obviously, this shot will not result in much distance; however, it is the safest shot to make sure that your next shot is from the fairway grass rather than to be hitting another shot from the sand.

If the ball rests in a greenside bunker, you may choose to chip the ball from the sand or hit an "explosion" shot. The decision will depend upon the depth of the bunker, the position of the ball in the sand, and the lip or "brow" of the bunker between the ball and the green. If the lip or brow is relatively low, a short iron (8 or 9) can be used to make a chipping stroke which will elevate the ball out of the bunker and carry it on a relatively low trajectory to the surface of the green where it will roll toward the hole. All of the mechanics that were described and illustrated in Chapter 4 are to be utilized on this stroke, i.e., weight on the left side with very little body motion as the arms are pushed away and brought back toward the ball. (See Figure 7-16.) You should not make any conscious effort to lift the ball with the hands or arms. Remember that the lofted clubface

will allow you to strike the lower half of the ball before contacting the sand. To get maximum distance out of the sand, you must contact the ball before the sand. (See Figure 7-14.)

If the fairway bunker is a foot or so lower than the surrounding area or if the ball is slightly buried, you may need to take a lofted club such as an 8, 9, or wedge so that you can intentionally strike the sand an inch or two behind the ball so that the ball can be

The Innisbrook Golf Institute
Innisbrook Resort
Tarpon Springs, FL

The Woodlands Golf Acadamy
The Nemacolin Woodlands Resort
Farmington, PA

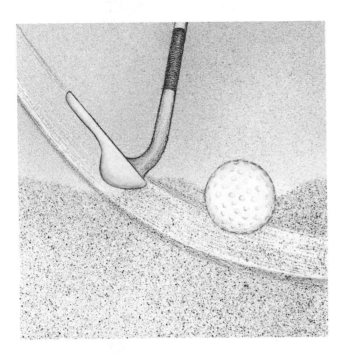

Fig. 7-15. When Ball is Setting in Sand, it can be Exploded by Striking the Sand an Inch or Two Behind the Ball.

clubface will elevate the ball out of the sand if you make the regular chipping stroke which descends toward the back of the ball as the clubface contacts the ball first and then the sand. The ball needs to be positioned more nearly opposite your right foot for this "bump and run" stroke. If you allow your body to sway or allow your right hand to take over the stroke on the way back to the ball, the clubface will enter the sand before it gets to the ball and the chipping stroke will be decelerating at impact. Under certain conditions you may elect to roll the ball out of the trap with the putter. You must remember that the rules of golf do not allow you to touch the sand with the club head until the stroke is made. Positioning the ball back in your stance and nearer a point that is perpendicular to the right foot will allow you to contact the ball without hitting the sand first on a chipping or putting stroke.

In deep greenside bunkers or when the ball is sitting "down" in the sand, it will be necessary to "explode" the ball out of the sand. When you are executing this stroke, the club head enters the sand at a point from

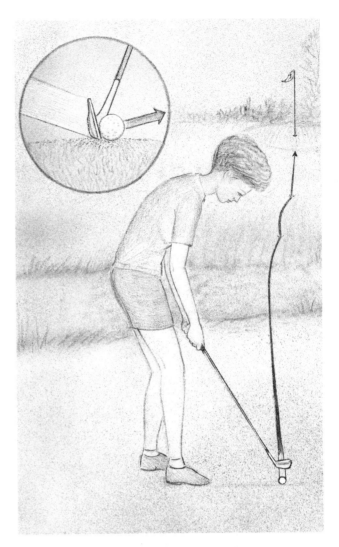

Fig. 7-16. A Chipping Stroke Can Be Made From Sand; Keep Body Still as Arms Move Club Away From and Back to the Ball.

two to three inches behind the ball and continues under the ball in a manner that allows the ball to ride out on a sliver of sand as the club head moves under the ball and exits the sand approximately three or four inches in front of where the ball was positioned. (See Figure 7-17.) The most important thing to remember about an explosion shot is that it is a three-quarters to full shot. Therefore, you will need to anchor your feet firmly in the sand. If your feet are about one inch below the surface, the club head should enter the sand behind the ball without any extra effort on your part. The three-quarter or full swing is necessary to create sufficient force to pull the club head through the sand.

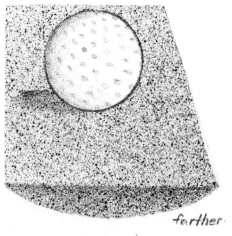

farther

slivers of sand

Shorter

Fig. 7-17. An Explosion Shot Carries the Ball Out
on a Sliver of Sand.

If there is insufficient force to pull the club
through the sand, the ball is likely not to be
carried out of the sand bunker. Even though
the explosion shot is a full shot, the alignment is a modification from the standard full
swing. When taking your stance for this
stroke, "open" your stance by pulling the left
foot back from the toe line that is parallel to

Fig. 7-18. The Ball Position Determines the Amount
of Sand to be Exploded and the Distance
the Ball Will Fly.

the target line. With this open stance, the
club is pushed away from the ball on the
target line. The ball position should be
slightly left of center, as the club will enter
the sand at or about the mid-point between
your feet. If the ball is setting down in the
sand, the ball should be right of the mid
point between your feet and the hands several inches in front of the ball. Conversely, if
you want to move less sand, position the ball
forward and have your hands slightly behind the ball. (See Figure 7-18.) In addition,
the clubface should be open, which means
that the face will be pointing up and to the
right of your target line. With your feet in an
open position, the target line is outside the
imaginary new line of your feet pointing left
of the target line that was created as you pull
the right foot away from the target line into
an "open" stance. This *outside* to *in* path of
the club head allows the ball to come out of
the sand on a higher trajectory and land
softly on the putting surface. This action
causes the club head to slice through the

sand on a slight "right to left" path. (See Figure 7-19.) This path and the open clubface at address help to prevent the inadvertent closing of the clubface which would make it more difficult to get the clubface under the ball and through the sand. Since the rules of golf do not permit you to touch the sand with your club prior to making the stroke, you should pre-set the clubface in an open position. Make a practice swing or two in the grass before walking into the bunker for the "explosion" shot. (See Figure 7-20.)

Fig. 7-19. The Outside-to-Inside Swing Path Explodes the Ball Out Safely.

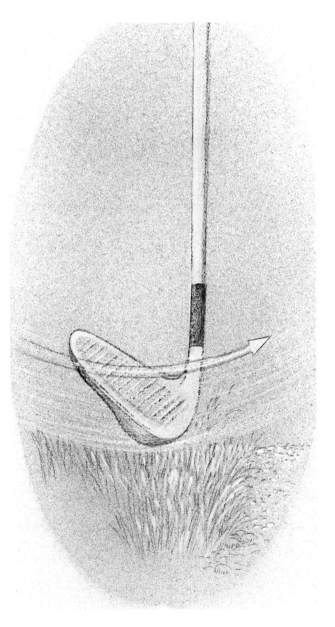

Fig. 7-20. Pre-set the Clubface Open and Take Practice Swing Before Entering Sand Trap (Bunker).

NOTES

NOTES

CHAPTER 8

STROKING WITH FAIRWAY WOODS

The stroke that is made with a wood club from the fairway is more of a sweeping stroke than the stroke made with middle or short irons that approach the ball from a steeper angle. The fairway woods are typically numbered 2, 3, 4, and 5. Some beginners and high handicapped players also use the more lofted fairway woods numbered 6 through 9 because they feel more confident with the larger head mass and the sweeping stroke than they do with an iron club when trying to carry the ball distances beyond 120 yards. The lower numbered woods have a straighter or more perpendicular clubface and a longer shaft than the higher numbered fairway woods. As confusing as it may be, a beginning player must realize that technology has caused fairway woods to be manufactured from material other than wood. As a result, we get such confusing terms as "metal woods." The description and illustration of this particular fairway stroke applies to the type of club being used rather than the material from which it might be made, i. e., wood, metal, or plastic.

Because of the limited amount of loft and the longer shaft on the 2 wood, I suggest that the beginning and high handicapped golfer concentrate on the fairway woods, 3, 4, 5, and 7. These clubs enable a player to stroke the ball in a manner which will get the ball airborne with sufficient force to roll

for quite some distance after it hits the ground. These clubs are used when distance is more of a premium than pinpoint accuracy.

Even though the principles described and illustrated in Chapter 6—The Full Swing—are those utilized with the fairway wood stroke, there are variations caused by the length of the shaft and the angle of the clubface as you move from the 3 wood to the higher numbered woods with shorter shafts and a more lofted face. As a result of the longer shaft, the 3 wood can be played several inches to the left of a line perpendicular with the middle of your stance while a 7 wood may be played at the mid-point of your stance or on a perpendicular line extending from the center of your stance. As with the iron strokes, the "right" ball position for a given individual will be determined by the extent to which the lower body shifts to the left in the down swing. The higher numbered woods with the shorter shaft and more lofted clubface will be pushed away from the ball on a steeper angle and will come back down to the ball on a steeper descending angle. (See Figure 8-0.)

Because of the longer shaft, the club is pushed away from the ball on the imaginary target line further before the club moves upward than is the case with the stroke made with the middle and short irons. Keep-

Fig. 8-0. The Fairway Wood is Struck with Slightly Descending Stroke

ing the club head closer to the ground for a longer period in the takeaway causes the swing to have a wider arc as the club head travels more nearly parallel to the ground immediately before, during, and after contact with the ball. (See Figure 8-1.) In part

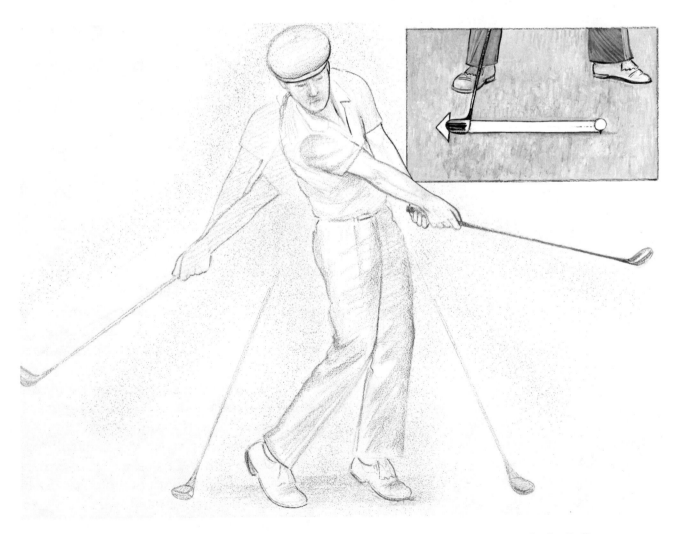

Fig. 8-1. The Fairway Wood Requires a Wide Arc Away From and Through the Ball.

because of the longer shaft, it is especially important for you to make a distinct pause at the top of the backswing before you begin to pull the club head back toward the ball. As with any full swing, you initiate the swing with the knees and lower body moving to the left. (See Figure 8-2.) After initiating lower body action the left shoulder and arm pull the club back into position to strike the ball.

Obviously, the sequence of motions in the full golf swing are not simple. Careful attention must be given to the components of the swing and these components must be linked together to produce a smooth, coordinated swing from takeaway to follow through. The full swing techniques are complex, and they do require careful attention to detail in order to achieve full understanding. Further, because the full swing involves all parts of the body, a considerable amount of repetition is involved in order to create the neuromuscular pattern necessary to produce the correct sequence of motions in a consistent manner. A great deal of practice is involved in order to acquire a smooth and coordinated swing. In the beginning you need to be very conscious of the various parts of the swing in order that each series of motions is made correctly. However, you need to move as soon as possible to the linking of different body motions together in order to create the smooth and coordinated swing.

Remember that the speed of the takeaway and completion of the back swing has little to do with the force applied to the ball. Therefore, you can be much more deliberate in your back swing than in the forward swing. The back swing creates potential energy through the coiling or turning process which is later imparted to the ball through the head of the golf club. It is important to emphasize that the fairway wood stroke, as in all other golf strokes, is an accelerating stroke from the top of the back swing all the way through impact of club head and ball.

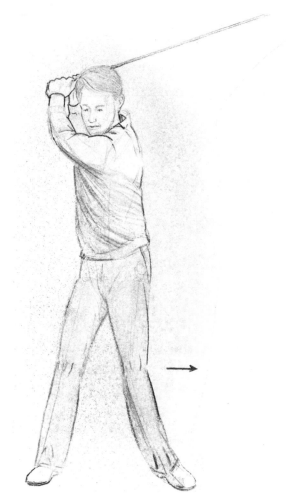

Fig. 8-2. The Lower Body Moves Forward as the Head and Upper Body Stay Behind the Ball.

SPECIAL FAIRWAY WOODS

In recent years, alterations have been made in the sole of the fairway wood to enable you to pull the club head more easily through longer grass in areas designated as "rough." One of these variations has a slightly thicker and v-shaped sole plate that allows the club to cut through high grass and get the full face of the club on the ball even though it is resting down in the taller grass. This club, although manufactured by several different companies, is generically referred to as a "ginty." Another type of variation has a sole plate with one-quarter-inch-high ridges perpendicular to the club face. (See Figure 8-3.) This variation is also

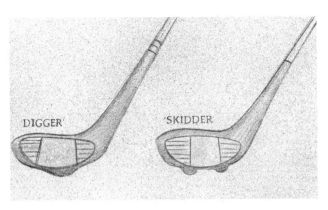

Fig. 8-3. Variations of the Fairway Wood Help to get the Ball Airborne From Rough.

designed to enable the club head to move down through longer grass which allows more of the clubface to contact the ball. Also the lower center of gravity of these modified fairway woods helps to get the ball on a higher trajectory.

As mentioned previously, the beginner and high handicap golfer may find it advantageous to utilize the more lofted fairway woods such as the 6, 7, and 8 rather than to use the longer irons. Because the 6, 7, and 8 woods have shorter shafts and a greater amount of loft built into the face of the club, than the 3 and 4 woods, the arc of the full swing will be more nearly circular than the more elliptical stroke made with the longer shafted fairway woods. Likewise, this more circular stroke will cause the 6, 7, and 8 woods to be delivered to the ball in a more descending stroke rather than the typical fairway wood stroke which is more of a sweeping action. Therefore, the ball will need to be positioned more nearly in the middle of your stance for the 6, 7 and 8 woods. (See Figure 8-4.)

It is important for you to remember that repetition is important for skill development. It does take practice to build a consistent and effective golf swing. However, proper techniques and body motions are essential to effective practice. Practicing incorrect techniques and body motions will also develop neuromuscular patterns that must be unlearned and exchanged for cor-

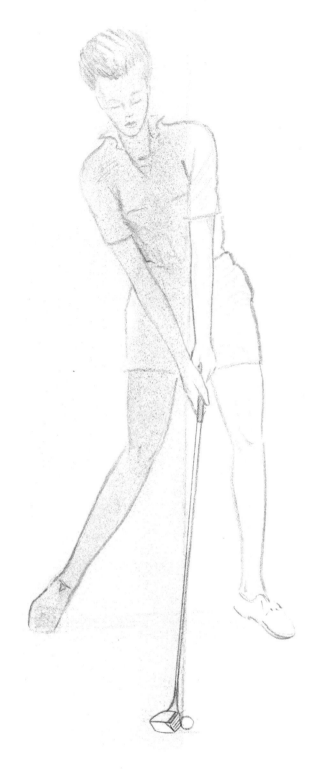

Fig. 8-4. For the Shorter Woods, the Ball Needs to be Positioned Near the Middle of Your Stance.

rect motions. Obviously, it is much more efficient for you to learn the correct motions initially rather than to go through the process of unlearning incorrect motions.

NOTES

NOTES

NOTES

CHAPTER 9

THE TEE SHOT

When play is initiated from the teeing ground or tee box, one may use a wooden or plastic *tee* that has a concave top on which the ball is mounted. On par four and par five holes you will be attempting to carry the ball as far as possible with your tee shot. Therefore, you would use one of the longer clubs with a relatively large club head. The club selected for the tee shot would normally be the number 1 (with 11 degrees of loft), number 2 (with 13 degrees of loft), or number 3 (with 15 degrees of loft) woods or a comparable club made from metal which has the same head shape as the more traditional wooden club. The 1 wood is referred to as the *driver*; however, the 2 and 3 woods are also used frequently for the tee shot. Because the 2 and 3 woods have a shorter shaft and more loft in the face, you may find that you get more satisfactory results with these clubs than with the driver in hitting the tee shot. You may sacrifice a bit of distance by using the 2 or 3 wood; however, you will typically find that you have better accuracy with a club that has a shorter shaft and a more lofted face than with the 1 wood.

The primary purpose of the tee shot is to carry the ball out onto the fairway as far as possible in order to have a shorter shot to the green. However, the longer shot is of little help if it is sliced right or pulled left into high grass, sand, or water which makes your second shot difficult to execute. The driver is the longest club, and it also has the smallest degree of loft. Because of these two factors the full swing techniques described and illustrated in Chapter 6 must be executed with a higher degree of precision in order to have a successful stroke. For these reasons, beginners and high handicap golfers are encouraged to use a number 2 or number 3 wood when taking the initial stroke from the teeing area on par 4 or 5 holes when distance rather than pinpoint accuracy is the primary concern. After you have achieved a relatively high level of consistency with the number 2 or number 3 wood from the tee, you may want to begin practicing with the driver.

The tee shot, by virtue of having the ball elevated on a tee, is played forward in your stance near a point that is perpendicular from the instep of your left foot. (See Figure 9-1.) If you are able to move your lower body to the left as you initiate the down swing with the driver or one of the fairway woods, the club will be approaching the ball on a path that is traveling parallel to the ground or slightly ascending. To maximize distance you should take advantage of the longer shaft by pushing the club head straight back from the ball (12 to 18 inches) with the muscles of the left side of your chest, the left shoulder and arm. Keeping the club

Fig. 9-1. With the Ball on a Tee, Position it on a Line Perpendicular With the Left Instep.

low in the takeaway helps to keep the left arm straight, widens your arc and helps you make a fuller turn. (See Figure 9-2.)

On par 3 holes which are typically no longer than 200 yards in length, you will be using a long iron or one of the shorter and more lofted woods such as the 7, 8, or 9. Even though you are allowed to use a wooden or plastic tee for this stroke, it is recommended that the tee be inserted so that the ball is no more than approximately 1/4 inch above the surface. This elevation of the ball for this stroke is similar to that which you would have for the same club when you execute the shot from fairway grass. The theory here is that you are going to strike the ball with a somewhat descending stroke, and the leading edge of the clubface should be able to strike the back of the ball and continue into the grass beneath the ball. Out in the fairway the close cropped grass elevates the ball naturally to this level; therefore, the tee shot with an iron should be in approximately the

same position as it would be if one were to execute the stroke from the fairway. Likewise, the tee shot struck with an iron or the more lofted fairway woods would be located at a point perpendicular to the mid-point of your stance as opposed to being teed more forward as was suggested for the 1, 2, and 3 woods.

When making the tee shot with 1, 2, or 3 wood and positioning the ball forward in your stance, the ball will be elevated on the tee to a point where approximately one-half to one-third of the diameter of the ball will be above the club head as it is positioned on the ground behind the teed ball. (See Figure 9-3.) The reason for this difference is that the clubs with a higher number have a greater degree of loft in the clubface. Since the number 1 wood or driver has the smallest degree of loft in the clubface, it is teed a bit higher in order to increase the trajectory of the ball when the stroke is made. As the sweeping stroke is made, the club head is gradually ascending as it reaches the ball. As a result, a more satisfactory combination of trajectory and length is achieved. Since the number 2 and number 3 woods have more loft built into the face of the clubs, a satisfactory trajectory can be achieved with a lower tee position. Even though the ball is teed somewhat lower, the tee shot with a more lofted wood is somewhat of a sweeping stroke like you would make with the fairway wood. When the more lofted wood clubs, such as the number 2 or number 3, are used to make the initial stroke from a tee, you may want to position the ball slightly more to the right of a line leading perpendicular toward your left instep because the shaft is shorter and you will have teed the ball slightly lower. If you were to tee the ball only slightly above the ground, you would place the ball in approximately the same position as for a fairway wood shot.

Some individuals prefer to make the tee shot with a 1 or 2 iron rather than the driver because they believe that they can strike the ball straighter and more consis-

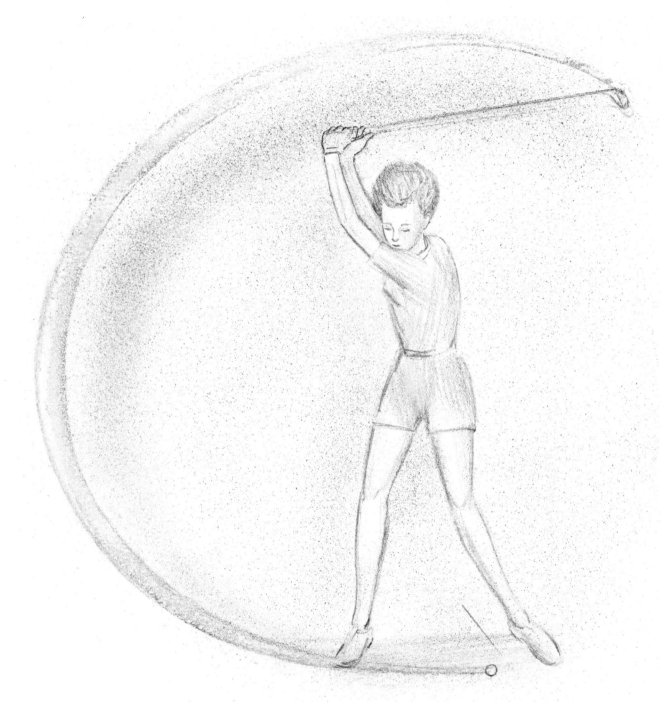

Fig. 9-2. Push the Club Back Low to Widen the Arc and Initiate A Big Shoulder Turn.

tently. As you may recall, it was suggested in Chapter 7 that the longer irons not be used by the beginning or high handicapped golfer. However, that suggestion was offered because of the greater difficulty in hitting these longer irons from the fairway. By being able to put the ball on a tee you may be able to make the tee shot more accurately and consistently with the number 1 and 2 irons than with the driver. Since the number 1 and 2 irons are approximately the same length as the number 3 wood, there will be very little difference in the ball placement and the swing plane needed when using these clubs for the tee shot.

Fig. 9-3. Proper Tee Position for the Driver has Approximately One-half to One-third of the Diameter of the Ball Above the Driver Face.

ALIGNMENT

Alignment is important when executing any of the strokes of golf. However, you need to be especially sensitive to aligning your body and the intended target line from the teeing area. The golf course architect frequently aligns the teeing area to the right or the left of the center of the fairway. Likewise, the grounds crew that mows the tee box may intentionally or inadvertently set the tee markers in an alignment that is not directly centered on the fairway. Because of these factors you need to be especially sensitive to aiming the ball and your body toward your intended target regardless of the configuration of the tee box or the tee markers. The rules of golf allow you to place the ball on a tee or on the ground any place within a rectangle bounded by the tee markers in front and a parallel line located no more than two club lengths from an imaginary line drawn between the two tee markers. Your feet may be outside this rectangular area, but the ball must be within the rectangle. (See Figure 9-4.)

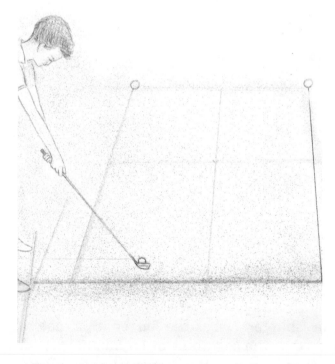

Fig. 9-4. For the Tee Shot, the Ball Must be Located Within the Designated Area.

104

Pebble Beach Golf Links
Pebble Beach, CA

The Grand Cypress Academy
of Golf
Grand Cypress Resort
Orlando, FL

It is recommended that you not use plastic tees to hold the ball if you are using a wooden club for your tee shot. The reason for this suggestion is that the harder material in the plastic tee can cause scratches in the finish of the wooden club. This admonition would not apply to clubs made from metal which would themselves be harder than the plastic material from which the tee might be made. However, regardless of their affect on wooden club heads, plastic tees cause more rapid dulling of mower blades.

NOTES

CHAPTER 10

INSTRUCTION: GOLF SCHOOLS AND ACADEMIES

Golf is a game for a lifetime. The surroundings in which the game is played adds to the game's appeal and a player's enjoyment. You can play or practice the strokes of golf in isolation or with friends as a social experience. However, the basic techniques of the game must be understood if you are to build a level of skill that will enable you to experience the positive rewards rather than the negative frustrations of inconsistency. This instructional manual is based on the principles of adult learning and can lead you to the level of competence essential for self satisfaction and enjoyment.

As mentioned in Chapter 1, which you may wish to review from time to time, the development of psychomotor skills requires that you (1) know and understand the correct physical movement, (2) execute these movements correctly with the help of a knowledgeable observer to be certain that the movements are being executed properly, and (3) practice the physical movements until they become a neuromuscular habit. With this understanding of the process of skill development, it is obvious that reading an instruction manual is only one step leading to skill development. As part of the process, it is important for you to know and understand the movements involved in each of the four strokes in the game of golf. The descriptions and illustrations presented in Chapters 2 through 9 will enable you to gain this base of knowledge and understanding. The execution of these movements need to be learned under the skillful eye of an effective instructor. This phase of your development will take several months for even the most dedicated learner. After you have gained knowledge and understanding and learned to execute the movements correctly, you will need to repeat these movements until they become a thoroughly established habit. You must be willing to make the investment of time for practice as well as money for instruction if you are to make continual progress to a satisfactory level of competence. There is no "quick fix"; skill development takes time.

SELECTING AN EFFECTIVE INSTRUCTOR

All individuals who provide golf instruction are not equally effective for all learners. It is important that you select an instructor who can relate to the techniques that you have studied in Chapters 2 through 9. These techniques have been presented in this manual after a through study of the techniques presented by the most knowledgeable golf teaching professionals in the United States. Obviously, individual teaching professionals will differ in their emphasis and in the vocabulary they use to describe and reinforce the movements essential to the successful execution of the four basic strokes of golf. Nevertheless, the most effective professionals will seek to reinforce the movements described and illustrated in Chapters 2 through 9. The movements involved in the several strokes of golf, especially the full swing, are complex. Your knowledge and thorough understanding are important; therefore, you need the reinforcement of demonstration and observation by an effective instructor. Analytical observation is especially important since you may not be making the physical movements that you understand and intend to make. An effective instructor understands the movements thoroughly and is sufficiently analytical in determining incorrect or even counterproductive movements.

Effective instructors use a variety of visual aids to enhance communication. One of the most effective teaching and learning tools is the video camera and play back unit. Beyond understanding and the ability to analyze a learner's movements, it is essential that your instructor be able to communicate with you in a meaningful way. Instructors who cover you with words or whose golf jargon does not convey meaning to you as a learner will not be helpful as you try to make the proper movements and develop a level of skill which will enable you to gain satisfaction from the game.

An instructor who will be most effective in helping you develop your golfing competencies will be able to help you establish long term goals as well as short range objectives for each lesson. Each lesson should lead to achievement and a basis for repetition that will facilitate your skill development. It is important for both you and your instructor to recognize that skill development is a gradual process in which one set of body positions and movements provides a basis for others. If some of the fundamentals (grip, stance, alignment, posture, and balance as discussed in Chapter 2) are not executed correctly, skill development will be adversely affected.

Even when instruction is effective and the learner is persistent and active, learning plateaus will occur. There will be stages in your development when progress seems to be slow or nearly nonexistent. This phenomenon is natural in the skill development process, and it occurs at different times and continues for different periods for different individuals. An effective instructor will facilitate your movement through plateaus and assist you in continuing your skill development.

Consider the possibility of contracting with your PGA professional for a series of lessons over a span of time. Ask if he or she is willing to answer questions and check your thought patterns or mechanics between lessons. If the PGA professional's schedule does not permit such attention, you may want to consider another professional.

Finally, to state the obvious, you must have a considerable amount of respect for and trust in your instructor. Some of your trust level will come as a result of your observation of his or her effectiveness in executing the various strokes of golf. However, the highest level of trust results from your progress as a learner. Your instructor's success as a player may present some immediate or early credibility; however, if you do not make progress, an instructors's success as a player is not very meaningful to you as a student.

PRACTICE FOR SKILL DEVELOPMENT

As indicated earlier in this chapter, skill development requires repetition (practice) to build consistent neuromuscular patterns. This manual and direct instruction provided by a qualified professional give you the essential information, including movements to be made, that provide direction and purpose for practice. A thorough understanding of the *static* and *dynamic* aspects of the golf strokes allows practice to be meaningful, thus leading to skill development. No benefit is derived from the repetition of incorrect body movements. In fact, an incorrect neuromuscular pattern is difficult to unlearn and replace with similar, yet different movements. Therefore, you need to have a relationship with your instructor that will allow a 10 to 15 minute check-up between lessons. In this way your execution of the movements emphasized in a previous lesson can be monitored with any necessary corrections to assure meaningful repetition on the practice range.

Research in psychomotor skill development has found that several short practice sessions are more productive than fewer marathon sessions. Not only do long practice sessions lead to fatigue and result in poorly executed body movements, but a learner's concentration diminishes, which also leads to incorrect execution. Practice sessions involving several different strokes with different clubs help to add interest, increase concentration, and minimize the fatigue factor. Long practice sessions that focus on one stroke often have negative effects. Hitting fewer balls thoughtfully, using the pre-swing routine each time, will be more helpful than randomly hitting buckets of balls. Remember: Always have a target for each practice ball.

Maximize your practice time by having a specific objective or purpose, e.g. 40 yard pitch shots with the pitching wedge in which five of ten balls end up no farther than five yards from the target and no more than one ball ends up farther than ten yards from the target. A practice session can have more than one objective, but each should specify (1) the type of stroke to be practiced, (2) the club to be used, and (3) the expected level of performance. Remember that certain body movements can be practiced without striking balls. An observer, a mirror or a video camera can be very helpful in monitoring as you practice specific body movements. Small plastic "whiffle" balls can be used when you do not have a large open area in which to practice. It is helpful to customize your

practice station by marking *target line*, *toe line*, and *ball position* (in relation to your left and right foot). This can be done with spray paint, wooden strips, or clubs. (See Figure 10-1) You must have the correct foundation (See Chapter 2) before a proper stroke can be made. A 24-inch wooden 2 × 4 or similar shaped object placed two inches outside the target line will let you know if you are swinging outside the target line as you return the club to the ball. Also, a club shaft placed outside your right foot will give you feedback if you are swaying too far to the right as you complete your backswing. (See Figure 10-2.)

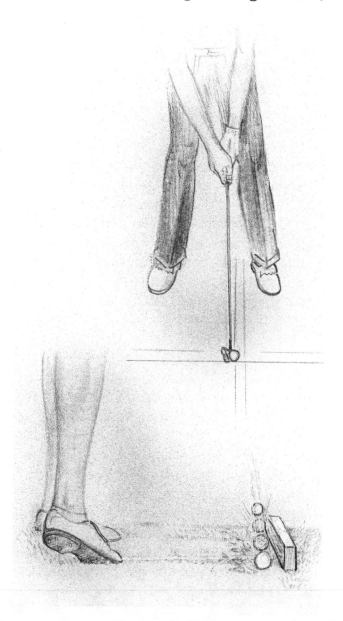

Fig. 10-1. Customize Practice Area for Proper Alignment and Ball Position

Fig. 10-2. A Club Shaft Inserted Opposite Right Leg Will Identify Body Sway in the Backswing.

You must practice the correct movements to create positive neuromuscular patterns that contribute to skill development. The long pitching stroke is a mini-swing that needs to be mastered before success with the full swing can be expected. It is important to do it right. If you have to make a half swing at three-quarters speed to do it correctly, then do just that. Learn to make the movements correctly; then learn to make them faster and more powerfully.

GOLF SCHOOLS AND ACADEMIES

At some point in your process of learning the fundamentals of golf, your progress and level of enjoyment can be expedited by your attendance at a 3 to 5 day intensive golf school or academy. Reputable golf schools offer instruction, supervised practice, and varied playing experiences. This experience is not recommended for an individual who has not acquired the fundamental knowledge and techniques inherent in the four basic strokes of golf. Intensive instruction, practice, and playing experiences can be much more beneficial if they are built upon a learner's knowledge base and sound stroke techniques even if those techniques are not well developed or being executed correctly.

An intensive period of instruction, practice, and supervised playing provided through a golf school or academy can enable a learner to speed up the development process in a significant way. To maximize this concentrated learning and development experience, you must prepare both your mind and your body. Be *mentally prepared* by reviewing the techniques involved in putting, chipping, pitching, and the full swing with both irons and woods. Make a list of points that are not clear, as well as movements that you have difficulty executing. Be *physically prepared* by doing the exercises described and illustrated in Chapter 2. By stretching and straining your muscles for several weeks in advance of your attendance at a school or academy, you will avoid some of the body soreness and fatigue that can seriously impede your psychomotor development on the second and third day of the intensive program.

Choosing a Golf School or Academy. There are tremendous variations among golf schools and academies. Some of them emphasize the social and accommodation features more than others. Obviously, factors such as climate, natural surroundings, resort atmosphere, social atmosphere, and room and meal accommodations are more important to some individuals than others. However, if one of your primary objectives in such an experience is to make substantial progress with your golfing development, you need to focus attention on (1) the experience and credentials of the teaching staff, (2) the instructional procedures utilized, (3) the ratio of instructors to students, (4) the experience of other individuals attending the school or academy, and (5) the concern expressed in you and your objectives by the director and other school personnel. This latter feature can be discerned by a request that you provide advance information about yourself and your golfing objectives. Also, there should be an indication of the willingness of the school or academy to adjust its instructional program to the differing experiences and skill levels of participants.

In the process of developing this manual there were interactions with dozens of teaching professionals and numerous golf schools and academies. To assist you in identifying one or more golf schools and academies which you might enjoy attending, a brief description of ten are provided for your review. These schools and academies selected for inclusion are not intended to be comprehensive, since there are more than 50 nationally advertised golf schools and academies with more than 75 locations in the United States. (See Appendix A.) However, each of the schools and academies listed in this manual are judged to be reputable and effective for knowledgeable beginners and high handicap players interested in making an investment to improve their skill levels. The omission of a school or academy does not signal either poor quality or inappropriateness for a beginner or inexperienced golfer. Some of the most highly advertised schools and academies have not been included because of their high cost and limited benefit to a beginner and inexperienced high handicap player. The quality of instruction is quite good, but not better than the more moderately priced schools and academies described in this chapter. Therefore, no one school or academy is best for every individual. Among the factors that you need to consider are:

1. Teacher/Student Ratio

a. The fewer students per teacher, the better, with 1 to 6 being a practical upper limit
b. Grouping of students by levels, e. g. beginners (1 year or less); high handicap players (30 +) with more than 1 year experience; high handicap (20-29); intermediate handicap (12-19); low handicap (8-11); and advanced player with handicap 0-7.

2. Instruction/Practice Facilities

a. Multiple station driving range, practice greens for chipping and putting, sand bunkers
b. Several golf holes dedicated to instruction (playing lessons)
c. Covered area in the event of showers

3. Credibility

a. Secure names of individuals in your area who have attended and ask questions
b. Inquire about the teaching credentials of instructor(s)

4. Instructional Program

a. Advanced analysis of player's level through questionnaire
b. Program geared to player's level
c. Combination of theory via film, demonstration and interaction, with supervised execution of mechanics and supervised practice
d. Include putting, chipping, pitching, full swing and bunker play
e. Utilize video technology

f. Balanced mix of watching, doing, listening, and interacting for no more than six hours per day

5. Course Access

a. Access to an eighteen-hole course at or near the school or academy is a plus; however, for a beginner (1 year or less) or high handicap player (30 +), this should be of low priority except for playing lessons. Using the relatively high cost time of a 3-5 day school or academy to play golf is not your best buy.

6. Cost

a. When comparing cost, it is recommended that you make a comparison chart with the variables that may or may not be included, e. g. meals and refreshments, lodging including non-golfing guests, green fees and cart fees, tax and gratuities, local transportation, travel costs

7. Additional Factors

a. Equipment analysis and specifications, prevailing weather conditions, travel time, availability of commuter sessions to reduce resort and other non-instructional costs, linkage with vacation plans

b. It is my judgement, however, that any of the golf schools or academies listed here are reputable and will provide you with meaningful and beneficial experiences. You may have noticed the beautiful color prints throughout this manual. Most of the color prints are identified with one of the golf schools or academies described in this chapter. They are all located in beautiful surroundings and provide an opportunity for a change of pace in a scenic environment with potential for increasing your level of competence and the resulting enjoyment that comes from higher levels of achievement.

THE FLORIDA GOLF SCHOOL

Location: Belleview-Biltmore Resort, Clearwater, FL; Lehigh Resort, Lehigh,FL; Sheraton Palm Coast Resort, Palm Coast, FL; Palm-Aire Spa Resort, Pompano Beach, FL; Indigo Lakes Resort, Daytona Beach, FL; and Cape Coral Resort, Ft. Myers, FL Telephone: (800) 364-6721

Director: Geoff Bryant, 2703 North Hwy. A 1 A, Suite D, Hutchinson Island, Fort Pierce, FL 34949

Session Lengths: Three-day school (Friday-Sunday or Monday-Wednesday) or five-day school (Monday-Friday)

Personnel: Selected PGA or LPGA trained instructors who are effective in the demonstration and communication of stroke principles in direct and simple terms. Instructors are screened on personal qualities such as patience, friendliness, positive attitudes and commitment to student improvement.

Facilities for Instruction and Practice: Each of the six locations have extensive range areas which provide for uncrowded practice and instruction of all golf strokes. Separate greens are available for learning the short game and putting.

Facilities for Playing: The courses at the six resort locations are among Florida's finest. They are well maintained which contributes to the enjoyment of the session as well as the beauty of the area. At Sheraton Palm and Palm-Aire there are four championship courses. The course at Indigo Lakes has been consistently rated among "Florida's Top Ten" by *Golf Week Magazine*. Beautifully manicured fairways, sculptured greens, strategically placed white sand bunkers, plus a choice of ocean and gulf views add to satisfaction with the session.

Instructional Program Features: The program groups students according to ability levels, including beginners. The program focus is on sound principles that simplify the mechanics of the golf swing. The management is committed to an instructional ratio of four students to one instructor. The five hours per day session has been found to be an appropriate length that is effective without being too tiring. The program provides an opportunity for on-course playing lessons which help participants take their swing from the practice tee to the course under playing conditions. No effort is made to force everyone's swing into the same mold. The instructional staff seek to take students where they are and improve their skills. Improvement is guaranteed. The program provides daily video taping, review, and critique sessions. These sessions provide the student with a clear direction for practice and improvement.

Accommodations: All locations provide deluxe resort guest rooms and the use of all resort facilities.

Relative Costs: The cost of the instructional program and accommodations range from $235 to $315 per day depending on one's choice of location. The program cost include lodging, all meals, video taping, greens fees and carts during and after class sessions, taxes and gratuities, and the use of all resort facilities.

Resort Features: All six locations are full service resorts with health centers, excellent cuisine, tennis courts, pools and beautiful surroundings. At the Sheraton Palm there is an 80 slip marina and a private beach on the Atlantic Ocean. The Belleview Biltmore features a new European health spa and overlooks the Edgewater Sand Key and the Gulf of Mexico. Each of the locations has unique and special features that you will want to consider as you make your choice.

THE WOODLANDS GOLF ACADEMY

Location: The Nemacolin Woodlands Resort, Farmington, Pennsylvania
Telephone: (412) 329-6900

Director: Greg Ortman, PGA

Session Length(s): The program is packaged as three full days or three half-day sessions. Special instructional sessions for business and corporate groups are arranged, and individual instruction is provided.

Personnel: Mr. Ortman utilizes PGA professionals from the area and visiting professionals who are invited for different three-day sessions.

Facilities for Instruction and Practice: The Academy has a large range for hitting full irons and woods. It also includes a covered area where instruction and practice can be continued in the event of inclement weather. There are separate greens for putting, chipping, and pitching as well as bunkers for instruction and practice. The practice area includes mounds for instruction and practice with "trouble" shots.

Facilities for Playing: The Woodlands Golf Course is a 6,600 yard, par 70, course located in the Pennsylvania Laurel Mountains. The course has rolling bluegrass fairways, bent grass greens with an appropriate combination of water hazards, sand, and grass bunkers.

Instructional Program Features: The instructional program is based on a uniquely prepared academy manual which covers the basic fundamentals of the golf swing based on research and professional experience. A low student-instructor ratio of four to one or less is maintained. Students are grouped by ability. The latest in computer and video technology is used to analyze and correct golf swing errors. The Academy specializes in equipment specification for participants. Minor adjustments in equipment, i. e., loft, lie, grips and swing weight are made on the spot to enhance instruction and learning. Specifications for custom clubs will be provided upon request. A careful analysis of a student's playing level and expectations are made prior to attendance, and the instructional program is customized to meet student needs.

Accommodations: Nemacolin Woodlands Resort offers luxurious accommodations—a variety of amenities and dining from casual to gourmet. Three breakfast meals are provided by the program. Academy participants have an option of choosing a room with a king-size bed, two beds (with or without whirlpool); one bed or two bed suites in the main lodge; or one or two bedroom condominiums.

Relative Costs: Moderately priced at $300 to $350 per day depending upon the accommodations chosen. Commuter rates are also available for individuals who do not choose to stay over night in the resort.

Resort Features: Nemacolin Woodlands Resort is a 550 acre spot of beauty in southwestern Pennsylvania which provides a vista of Maryland and West Virginia. This is a full service resort with facilities for tennis, swimming, fishing, hiking, and jogging. Its world class spa offers state-of-the-art exercise equipment and professionally administered treatments. The natural beauty of the area at all times of the year provides an inspiring environment as well as an excellent golf learning environment.

THE GRAND CYPRESS ACADEMY OF GOLF

Location: Grand Cypress Resort, Orlando, Florida
Telephone: (800) 835-7377

Director: Fred Griffin, Class-A PGA Professional

Session Length(s): Sessions are designed for two, three, three and half, and four day time periods.

Personnel: In addition to Mr. Griffin, the regular staff includes Dr. Ralph Mann, a specialist in biomechanics, and Mr. Phil Rogers, a Senior PGA Tour professional. Other PGA professional instructors supplement the regular staff.

Facilities for Instruction and Practice: The Academy of Golf at Grand Cypress has one of the best instruction and practice facilities available in the United States. The extensive range area provides an opportunity to have an uncrowded practice area for all shots. In addition there are four separate greens as well as nine bunkers in which to learn and practice sand shots. Also, as part of the Academy facilities, there are three holes designed by Jack Nicklaus which provide a variety of learning experiences. Each hole has four tee boxes, three flag positions, and sand bunkers which provide all the challenges of regular course play on three holes.

Facilities for Playing: Grand Cypress Golf Club has 45 holes of Jack Nicklaus designed golf. These courses offer not only the challenges one would expect of a course created by Nicklaus, but it provides a variety of visual treats as well. The most recent addition to the club is a Nicklaus rendition of the Old Course at Saint Andrews, Scotland. The cart paths, the pot bunkers, the mounds, the winding burns or creeks which are spanned by stone bridges, and seven large double greens clearly replicate Scotland's windswept links. The other courses are excellent Florida courses with sand, lakes, and elegant pines. The courses at Grand Cypress were voted among the top 25 of *Golf Digest's* ranking of the best resort courses in America.

Instructional Program Features: The program groups students according to ability levels and focuses on the techniques of the full swing as well as improvement of the short game skills of putting, chipping, pitching, and bunker play. A special feature of the instructional program is a computer model developed by Dr. Ralph Mann after analyzing the swings of more than 50 top PGA touring professionals. The computer model can be adjusted for different size and body type by comparing the PGA computer model with high resolution, slow motion video of the student's actual swing. The staff can accent strengths and correct weaknesses.

The student's full swing computer instruction takes place and is recorded right on the tee. The entire lesson is provided on a take-home video tape featuring the instructor's comments and the student's computer model superimposed on the actual swing. Each participant receives a specially designed Academy instructional notebook, computerized club fitting, unlimited use of the academy's practice holes and range, and supervised on-course instruction for the three and four day sessions. The program also includes one complimentary round of golf on one of the three Grand Cypress courses.

Accommodations: The program at the Grand Cypress Academy does not include accommodations. Participants at the Academy can be accommodated at the Grand Cypress Resort or they may choose other accommodations in the Orlando area where the full range of overnight and dining facilities are available from $50 to $300 per night depending on the season and degree of luxury desired.

Relative Costs: The instructional program is above average in cost as its $550 to $600 per day cost does not include accommodations.

Resort Features: Grand Cypress Resort is a world class resort of more than 1,500 acres. *Golf Magazine* awarded Grand Cypress Resort a gold medal as one of the finest golf resorts in America. Only 12 resorts throughout the United States received this award. The resort grounds have received awards by the American Society of Landscape Architects, the Florida Nurserymen and Growers Association, and the Landscape Contractors of America for the design, installation, and maintenance of the outdoor landscape and the atrium areas of the Hyatt Regency Grand Cypress Hotel. In addition to its beauty, Grand Cypress has all of the amenities that one would expect such as swimming, racquet sports, equestrian trails, nature areas, fitness centers, and the finest in dining facilities.

PINE NEEDLES LEARNING CENTER

Location: Pine Needles Resort, Southern Pines, North Carolina
Telephone: (919) 692-7111

Director: Dr. Jim Suttie, PGA

Session Length(s): Standard program of four and five day duration; for many years Pine Needles has featured *Golfaris* for women, men, couples, youth, and adults.

Personnel: Peggy Kirk Bell, owner of Pine Needles, is one of the most respected golf teachers in America and has been designated teacher of the year by the Ladies' Professional Golf Association. In Addition to Ms. Bell and Dr. Suttie, other PGA professionals such as Rob Strano, Tod Killian, Carol Johnson, Casey Johnstone and touring professional, Pat McGowan provide instruction.

Facilities for Instruction: The separate teaching and practice area features a unique covered practice tee which allows instruction and practice to continue uninterrupted by rain showers. Separate greens are available for practicing the short game and putting.

Facilities for Playing: The Pine Needles Resort has one of the most popular courses in the Pinehurst area—a par 71 layout designed by the legendary golf course architect, Donald Ross. Ross skillfully blended the gently rolling countryside into a masterpiece with nature.

Instructional Program Features: The director and staff are sensitive to differing abilities and provide group instruction separately for beginners, intermediate, or advanced players. The instructional program provides large group instruction related to the theory of the golf swing and the mental aspects of the game. Individual and small group instruction (not exceeding a four student to one instructor ratio) is designed to help you develop the necessary techniques to execute each of the four basic strokes (putting, chipping, pitching, and the full swing), as well as specialty shots involved in the game. The instructional program involves the use of multi-visual video techniques, computer graphics, side-by-side comparison of student and role model, and the most sophisticated visual and video techniques available for analyzing swing errors. There is considerable emphasis on learning through visual feedback as participants are video taped four times during the session. In addition to instruction on the four basic strokes and the trouble shots from uneven lies and sand, students are provided with special practice drills to assist with skill development. The program also provides opportunities for students to "take their game to the course" under the supervision of the teaching professionals. In addition to instruction, the program provides an opportunity for a physical fitness evaluation and specification for a physical training program as well as an evaluation of the student's equipment and specifications for making equipment modifications. Students leave the program with a full visual evaluation of their golf swing from four angles. The tape has audio-over voice with computer graphics and other specialized video techniques. The tape describes swing errors and drills to correct faults in a student's stroke.

Accommodations: The Pine Needles Resort offers high quality living areas, recreation, and dining accommodations for 140 guests. The lodges are nestled throughout a natural setting. Even though the setting is rustic, the accommodations can best be described as casual luxury.

Relative Costs: The instructional program and the accommodations are moderately priced at $250-$350 per day packages with instruction, lodging, meals, and golf included.

Resort Features: The resort has many non-golf related features such as a heated pool, tennis courts, exercise room, whirlpool, and sauna. The main lodge is a picture of southern elegance. The dining experiences at Pine Needles are superb. Pine Needles has meeting facilities to accommodate seminars, board meetings, and banquets. This resort has a tradition that dates back to an earlier era when warmth, charm, and gracious hospitality were a way of life. This legacy continues today at Pine Needles.

UNITED STATES GOLF ACADEMY

Location: Swan Lake Golf Resort, Plymouth, Indiana
   Telephone: (219) 935-5680

Director: Roger W. Swanson

Session Length(s): Three-day sessions on Monday through Wednesday or Friday through Sunday.

Personnel: In addition to the director, the Academy utilizes professionals who have been identified for their instructional effectiveness and ability to relate to a wide range of student ability from beginner to advanced amateur.

Facilities for Instruction and Practice: Extensive practice greens, bunkers, and a driving range are available for practicing all of the basic golf strokes. Also, there is a separate par 3 course used for supervised instruction.

Facilities for Playing: The resort has two 18-hole courses. The East course is dotted with lakes and streams which present a challenge for accuracy. The West course is less hazardous, but longer as it features large greens and wide fairways.

Instructional Program Features: The program provides personalized daily instruction with a ratio that does not exceed five students to one instructor. There are separate groups for men and women, as well as for beginners, intermediates, and advanced students. The program focuses on a three-hour block of daily instruction. The rest of the day is available for play or additional practice. Video tape swing analysis provides for corrective adjustments recommended by a students's instructor.

Accommodations: Students may choose the comfort of private motel accommodations or dorm-style living on the resort site with all meals included.

Relative Costs: Economically priced at $150 to $250 per day.

Resort Features: Swan Lake Golf Resort offers a relaxed and friendly atmosphere with a focus on golf. Casualness, but solid quality in a midwestern atmosphere are the by words at Swan Lake. This resort has a swimming pool, and there is good fishing in the area.

THE INNISBROOK GOLF INSTITUTE

Location: Innisbrook Resort, Tarpon Springs, Florida
Telephone: (813) 942-2000

Directors: Lew Smithers III, Director of Instruction and Jay Overton, Vice President of Golf Operation

Session Length(s): Four days/three nights programs (Thursday-Sunday or Sunday-Wednesday) are provided on a regular basis. Also a junior golf institute of six days and five nights duration is offered during the summer.

Personnel: In addition to Lew Smithers and Jay Overton, the institute employs additional PGA professionals to maintain a four students to one instructor ratio.

Facilities for Instruction and Practice: The instructional program is conducted on spacious range facilities with large greens for instruction and practice of putting, chipping, and pitching.

Facilities for Playing: Innisbrook has 63 great holes on three championship courses that are among the most beautiful in the country. The Copperhead, one of Florida's top rated courses, plays up to 7,031 yards on various combinations of three nines. The 7,000 yard Island Course calls for long, straight tee shots to avoid lakes and bunkers. The third course, Sandpiper, is the shortest at 6,000 yards; however, its rolling fairways are crisscrossed with streams and lakes which demand accuracy. The institute program includes one round of golf each day on one of these championship courses.

Instructional Program Features: The instructional program features a first-rate golf institute instruction manual. The instructional manual and the program focus on the fundamentals of the golf swing. The program features three to four hours of individual and small group instruction each day. The small group instruction is limited to four students for one instructor. Students are grouped according to skill level. The program recognizes the importance of goals set by participants. There is sufficient attention to the mental aspect of the game so that each student learns how and why things happen as they make a given golf stroke. Through their instructional program, and with the use of drills and exercises, a student can continue to learn and develop a sound golf swing. The program utilizes video tape in order that students can view their movements throughout the golf swing.

Accommodations: The program includes a luxurious club suite for three nights, personal locker, room service, club storage, and other related service charges. Even though breakfast and lunch are included in the program, the guest lodges have fully equipped kitchens.

Relative Costs: The program is moderately priced which ranges from $250 to $350 per day depending on the time of the year.

Resort Features: Innisbrook, a full-service, modern resort with special amenities, includes a racquet and fitness center. The Racquet Center is world class with a five-star rating; it includes 18 tennis courts and four indoor air-conditioned racket ball courts. There are six swimming pools, miles of roads and trails for jogging and cycling. The Fitness Center includes all types of modern fitness equipment, saunas, and whirlpools. The unique fishing village of Tarpon Springs with gulf fishing available is close to the resort. There are club houses at each of the three resort courses that provide outstanding cuisine.

The Copperhead
Innisbrook Resort
Tarpon Springs, FL

The Woodlands at The Nemacolin Resort
Farmington, PA

THE GOLF CLINIC

Location: Poppy Hills Golf Course, Pebble Beach, California
Telephone: 800 321-9401

Directors: John Geertsen Jr. and Ben Alexander

Session Length(s): A standard program is five days; however, modified programs of two, three, or four day durations can be arranged. Private group programs can be customized from one hour to two weeks.

Personnel: The instructional staff ranges from John Geertsen Jr., a private teaching professional and one of the directors, to Mike Reid, a tour professional. Other PGA professionals include Ed Oldfield, Ron Rhoads, John Geertsen Sr., Ben Alexander, and Jack Guio. Each season one or more visiting tour professionals such as Mike Reid and Johnny Miller join the staff for a special week. Other PGA and LPGA professionals from the area are utilized to maintain a ratio of no greater than four students to one professional. Chuck Hogan, founder of Sports Enhancement Associates (SEA) who has worked with countless international athletes including 22 PGA and LPGA tour players, shares his learning concepts in two chapters of the manual that each participant receives.

Facilities for Instruction and Practice: There are private range areas including practice greens, mounds, and bunkers for instruction and practice of all the basic strokes of golf and the short game. The program provides for the teaching staff to be with students for two different practice rounds at Spyglass Hill Golf Course and Pebble Beach Golf Links.

Facilities for Play: The Poppy Hills Golf Club, the site for the Golf Clinic, provides for twilight rounds on the three days when playing lessons with instructors are not scheduled. Poppy Hills, designed by Robert Trent Jones Jr., is one of many beautiful and challenging links courses in the Pebble Beach Forest. The setting in which Pebble Beach, Spyglass Hill, and Poppy Hills have been built is truly one of nature's most magnificent.

Instructional Program Features: The instructional program focuses on basic fundamentals of the golf swing. Considerable attention is given to individual full swing analysis to build and improve each person's swing. Video technology is provided with one hour and twenty minutes of instruction followed by one-on-one sessions with John Geertsen's audio analysis of each participant's swing. In-depth instruction is provided through the clinic's golf manual for continuation of the development process after the student returns home. Each student is taped and analyzed several times during the week as the process of swing development progresses. Each participant receives a personal video tape to review at home. The playing lessons emphasize how to "work the ball" on the course and important scoring techniques.

Accommodations: Through special arrangements, participants of the Golf Clinic spend Sunday through Friday at the elegant Pebble Beach Resorts. The program includes breakfast and lunch each day and dinner for three nights. There are provisions for commuters to participate with no accommodations provided and only lunch for Monday through Friday. Shortened programs can be arranged with accommodations in Monterey or Carmel.

Relative Costs: This is a higher than average cost program that can be customized from $110 an hour for private sessions to clinics ranging in price from $500 to $1,000 a day, depending on accommodations.

Resort Features: The world famous Pebble Beach Resorts are full service resorts with very luxurious accommodations. These resorts have swimming pools, health clubs, spas, tennis, and a full equestrian center with riding trails in the forests and on the beaches. These and other amenities have made this area one of the most preferred by golfers throughout the world.

VINTAGE GOLF SCHOOLS

Location: Port Royal Golf Club, Hilton Head Island, South Carolina
Telephone: (803) 681-2406

Director: Val Edwards

Session Length(s): The principal program consists of three full days or five full days of instruction; the school also offers a mini school (4 1/2 hours) on a daily basis, as well as private instruction by appointment. The amount of direct instruction for the three-day program is three hours per day, excluding supervised playing lessons. Corporate programs are provided throughout the United States.

Personnel: In addition to Keith Marks Sr., who is acknowledged by *Golf Magazine* as one of the country's finest teachers, the school hires other PGA professionals including Keith Marks Jr.

Facilities for Instruction and Practice: The school has an ample range for instruction and practicing all phases of the game. Separate greens and bunker areas are available to the school.

Facilities for Playing: Port Royal has three beautiful island courses. The program is designed with afternoon playing sessions on these courses under the supervision of a professional.

Instructional Program Features: The philosophy of Keith Marks is very evident in the program. The program focuses on the basics of posture, body mechanics, and the plane of the swing. These three factors are inherent in the system of teaching that allows any golfer, regardless of size, age, or build to develop a consistent and effective golf swing. The program features a three student to one teacher ratio which assures considerable personal attention. Lessons are video taped with state-of-the-art equipment for instant analysis by student and teacher. A video swing analysis is made of the four basic strokes of golf, and a personal written swing program with the video tape is the student's property to take home and review as the process of skill development continues.

Accommodations: The program provides lodging for three or five nights including breakfast and lunch.

Relative Costs: The school is moderately priced between $250 and $350 per day. Instruction can be provided on a commuter basis for one day at considerably less cost than the per day rate for the regular three- or five-day schools. In addition, hourly lessons can be provided.

Resort Features: Port Royal Golf Club, located on Hilton Head Island, offers three championship courses. Planter's Row was the site of the 1986 Seniors PGA Championship. The island location provides spectacular ocean views, white beaches, and pine forests. The Westin Resort Hotel has a five star rating with all the amenities associated with a world class resort (e.g., tennis courts, fitness center, seafood cuisine, and croquet).

THE ILLINOIS GOLF SCHOOL

Location: Eagle Ridge Inn and Resort, Galena, Illinois
Telephone: 800 892-2269

Directors: Bob Wyatt Jr. and Geoff Bryant

Session Length(s): Standard programs are offered on a five-day format, Monday-Friday; or a three-day format, Monday-Wednesday or Friday-Sunday.

Personnel: In addition to the two directors, the staff includes other PGA or USGTA prepared instructors sufficient to maintain a ratio of one instructor to four students.

Facilities for Instruction and Practice: Eagle Ridge has a large three-tee level range and separate practice greens, mounds, and bunkers for practice of all the basic strokes of golf, especially the short game. A special classroom and video area are provided for group instruction and individual analysis. On-course instruction is provided on either of the regular Eagle Ridge courses.

Facilities for Playing: Eagle Ridge provides two 18-hole courses that are rated among the best of the world's top golf resorts. The rugged natural terrain provides dense forested ridges and ravines between fairways. Natural rock outcroppings frame picturesque fairways that border Galena Lake. The program fee includes green fees and carts for playing in the late afternoon and evenings.

Instructional Program Features: The program is based on sound fundamentals of the static and dynamic aspects of the golf swing. This simplified approach helps all levels of players to improve noticeably each day. Strategic use of video tapes with stop action analysis is a key component of the instructional program. Supervised practice is recognized as an important element of skill development. On-course time with an instructor helps to take the techniques from the practice range to the course. Course strategy and decision making are recognized as important elements of better scoring, which leads to player satisfaction.

Accommodations: Participants stay at Eagle Ridge Inn, a New England style, 66 room modern facility with all the conveniences and amenities expected of a first-class resort. In addition, there are more than 200 condos, town houses, and villas available to golf school students. Lodging and all meals are included in the program costs.

Relative Cost: Moderately priced at $250 to $300 per day.

Resort Features: Eagle Ridge is located in the northwest corner of Illinois near the Wisconsin, Iowa, and Minnesota borders. The terrain is unlike the plains of the midwest. The 6,800 acre Galena Territory is composed of forests, lakes, rugged ridges, deep ravines, and rolling meadows. This full service resort has an indoor pool, facilities for boating or fishing, a fitness center, tennis courts, and horseback riding.

CRAFT-ZAVICHAS GOLF SCHOOL

Locations: Pueblo West Golf Club, Pueblo West, Colorado; Tucson National Golf and Conference Center, Tucson, Arizona; Telephone (719) 564-4449

Directors: Linda Craft and Penny Zavichas, LPGA Master Professionals

Session Length(s): Six to eight days in Colorado and Arizona

Personnel: In addition to the directors, a staff of experienced teaching "Class A" professionals are drawn from Colorado, Nebraska, Arizona, California, Texas, Washington, South Carolina, Iowa, and Minnesota.

Facilities for Instruction and Practice: All of these school sites have large range areas for instruction and practice on all of the golf strokes. This includes large practice greens and bunkers for practicing putting, chipping, pitching, and sand play. At Tucson National the practice facilities are outstanding. An indoor video analysis room is a special feature of this location. At Pueblo West there are also specially designed instruction and practice facilities.

Facilities for Playing: The Tucson location has a superb 27 holes of golf, and the program provides all green fees and carts for unlimited play after instruction. The Pueblo West Golf Course is a par 72 hole layout in the foothills of the Rocky Mountains. The program provides complimentary golf and cart for play on Pueblo West.

Instructional Program Features: The instructional program focuses on basic fundamentals of the golf swing with repetition and drills to help develop skill with each of the strokes of golf. In no case is the ratio of students to instructor greater than five to one. Students are grouped according to levels of beginner, intermediate, and advanced. Instruction is also separated for men and women students, with women instructors for women students and men instructors for men students. Considerable attention is placed on split screen, slow motion video analysis. Students are provided with a personal instruction manual and take home video tape. The program focuses on the proper execution of fundamentals and repetition under constant professional supervision. Five hours of instruction are provided each day on the practice facility and additional time is spent on course management and the mental aspects of the game.

Accommodations: At the Tucson site the lodging is in resort villas. At the Pueblo site, students stay at the Inn at Pueblo West. Lunch and some dinners are provided at these locations.

Relative Costs: The cost at the Pueblo West site is moderate at approximately $175 per day; the Tucson site is slightly more at approximately $285 per day. Commuter rates for instruction are also available.

Resort Features: The Tucson National Golf and Conference Center is a full service resort and spa that features hydrotherapy pools, special baths, massages, and many other outstanding features; Pueblo West is a low key western resort with an informal and relaxing atmosphere. This small resort which accommodates approximately 100 guests is located in the foothills of the Rocky Mountains and is at an altitude of nearly 5,000 feet.

Selected References

Bell, Peggy Kirk. *A Woman's Way To Better Golf*, New York: E. P. Dutton & Co., Inc., 1966.

Charles, Bob & Ganem, Roger P. *Left-Handed Golf*, Englewood Cliffs, N.J. : Prentice-Hall, Inc., 1965.

Coop, Richard; Wiren, G. & Sheehan, L. *The New Golf Mind*, New York: Simon & Schuster, 1978.

Demaret, Jimmy; Sarazen, Gene & Suggs, Louise. *Golf Magazine's Your Short Game*, New York: Harper & Row, 1962.

Ford, Doug. *Getting Started In Golf*, New York: Sterling Publishing, 1964.

Geiberger, Al & Dennis, Larry. *Tempo, Golf's Master Key, How to Find It, How to Keep It*, Norwalk, CT: Golf Digest, Inc., 1980.

Hebron, Michael. *See and Feel the Inside Move the Outside*, Smithtown, N.Y.: Private Publication, 1984.

Hebron, Michael. The Art and Zen of Learning Golf, Smithtown, N.Y.: Private Publication, 1990.

Johnson, Carol C. & Johnstone, Ann Casey. *Golf—A Positive Approach*, Reading, MA: Addison-Wesley Publishing Co., 1975.

Keogh, Barbara K. & Smith, Carol E. *Personal Par, A Psychological System of Golf for Women*, Champaign, IL: Human Kinetics Publishers, Inc., 1985.

Magill, Richard A. *Motor Learning. Concepts and Application*, Dubuque, IA: W. C. Brown, 1989.

Murphy, Michael. *Golf in the Kingdom*, New York: Dell Publishing Co., Inc., 1972.

Owens, De De & Bunker, Linda. Golf: Steps to Success, Champaign, IL: Leisure Press, 1989.

Pelz, Dave & Mastroni, Nick. *Putt Like the Pros*, New York: Harper & Row, 1989.

Player, Gary. *Golf Begins at Fifty*, New York: Simon and Schuster, 1988.

Snead, Sam & Stump, Al. *The Education of A Golfer*, New York: Simon & Schuster, 1962.

Toski, Bob; Love, Davis Jr. & Carney, Robert. *How To Feel A Real Golf Swing*, Trumbull, CT: Golf Digest, Inc., 1988.

Venturi, Ken & Barkow, Al. *The Ken Venturi Analysis*, New York: Atheneum, 1981.

Watson, Tom. *Getting Up and Down*, New York: Random House, 1983.

Wiren, Gary. *Golf: Building A Solid Game*, Englewood Cliffs, N.J.: Prentice-Hall. Inc., 1987.

Appendix A

A Partial List of Golf Schools and Academies in the United States

The Academy of Golf at the Hills of Lakeway
One World Square
Austin, TX 78738

The Academy of Golf
Grand Cypress Resort
1 North Jacaranda
Orlando, FL 32819

Arnold Palmer Golf School
9000 Bay Hill Boulevard
Orlando, FL 32910

Ben Sutton's Golf School
P. O. Box 9199
Canton, OH 44711

Berkshire School of Golf
Cranwell Resort
55 Lee Road
Lenox, MA 01240

Bertholy Method Golf School
Foxfire Village
Jackson Springs, NC 27281

Bill Skelley's Schools of Golf
Miami Lakes Inn & Golf Resort
Miami Lakes, FL 33014

Craft-Zavichas Golf School
600 Dittmer Avenue
Pueblo, CO 81005

The Exceller Golf Schools
3546 East Gold Dust Avenue
Suite One
Phoenix, AZ 85028

The Florida Golf Academy
720 Goodlette Road, Suite 303
Naples, FL 33940

The Florida Golf School
2703 N. Highway A1A, Suite D
North Hutchinson Island
Ft. Pierce, FL 34949

The Golf Institute
Rolling Hills Resort
3501 W. Rolling Hills Circle
Ft. Lauderdale, FL 33328

The Golf Clinic at Pebble Beach
P. O. Box M
Carmel, CA 93921

Golf Digest Instruction School
5520 Park Ave., Box 395
Trumbull, CT 06611

The Golf School
Grenelefe Resort
3200 State Road 546
Grenelefe, FL 33844-9732

The Golf School
Plantation Golf Resort
P. O. Box 1116
Crystal River, FL 32629

The Golf School
Mount Snow Resort
Mount Snow, VT 05356

Golf Schools of Scottsdale
Resort Suites
7677 E. Princess Blvd.
Scottsdale, AZ 85255

Golf University of the Midwest
Lodge of the Four Seasons
Lake Ozark, MO 65049

The Golf University at San Diego
2001 Old Hwy. 395
Fallbrook, CA 92028

The Illinois Golf School
Eagle Ridge Inn & Resort
U. S. Route 20, Box 777
Galena, IL 61036

Innisbrook Golf Institute
P. O. Drawer 1088
Tarpon Springs, FL 34688-1088

Jeri Reid's Golf School
2059 Southwest 15th Street
Deerfield Beach, FL 33442

Jimmy Ballard Golf Workshop
Doral Country Club
4400 N W 87th Avenue
Miami, Fl 33178

John Jacobs' Practical Golf School
7127 East Sahuaro, Suite 101
Scottsdale, AZ 85254

John Schlee's Maximum Golf School
4923 Avila Avenue
Carlsbad, CA 92008

La Costa Golf School
LaCosta Hotel and Spa
Carlsbad, CA 92008

Margo Walden Golf School
Seabrook Island Resort
P. O. Box 32099
Charleston, SC 29417

National Academy of Golf
490 Fourth Avenue South
Naples, FL 33940

Paradise Golf Schools
281 U. S. 27 North Village
Fountain Plaza
Sebring, FL 33870

Paul Tessler's Westgate Golf Center
3781 State Rt. 5
Newton Falls, OH 44444

Proformance Golf Schools
Orange Tree Golf Resort
Phoenix, AZ 85028

PGA National Golf School
1000 Avenue of the Champions
Palm Beach Gardens, FL 33418

Pinehurst Golf Advantage
Golf Advantage Teaching Center
P. O. Box 4000
Pinehurst Country Club
Pinehurst, NC 28374

Pine Needles Learning Center
Pine Needles Lodge & G. C.
Box 88
Southern Pines, NC 28387

Professional Golf Schools of America
815 S. U.S. #1, Suite 4
Jupiter, FL 33477

Quinzi Golf Teaching Center
3784 Hwy. 19 North
Palm Harbor, FL 34684

Roland Stafford Golf School
Kass Inn
Route 30
Margaretville, NY 12455

The Rirson Golf Studio
The Legends
P. O. Box 2219
Myrtle Beach, SC 29578-2219

Skinner Golf Schools
P. O. Box 1001
North Platte, NE 69101

Silver Sands Golf Academy
American Resort
1890 S. Shore Drive
Delavan, WI 53115

Sports Enhancement Associates (SEA)
P. O. Box 2788
Sedona, AZ 86336

Strand Golf Academy
1204 Linda Drive
Conway, SC 29526

The Stratton Golf School
The Stratton/Scottsdale Corporation
Stratton Mountain, VT 05155

Swing's The Thing Golf School
P. O. Box 200
Shawnee-On-Delaware, PA 18356

SyberVision Golf School
11 Maiden Lane, Suite 400
San Francisco, CA 94108

Trahan Golf School
Sea Pines Plantation
P. O. Box 7000
Hilton Head Island, SC 29938

U. S. Golf Academy
Swan Lake Resort
5203 Plymouth LaPorte Trail
Plymouth, IN 46563

Vintage Golf Schools
Port Royal Resort
P. O. Box 5045
Hilton Head, SC 29938

White Mountain Golf School
White Mountain Country Club
P. O. Box 83
Ashland, NH 03217

The Woodlands Golf Academy
Nemacolin Woodlands Resort
P. O. Box 188
Farmington, PA 15437

Appendix B

The Joy of Golf

by Dr. Gary Wiren

There are many sources of enjoyment available to a golfer other than "shooting a good round." Players who aren't aware of these opportunities, should be taught. The professional is the resident teacher. Here is an edited list of some of golf's joys written by master professional John Gerring:

"Why should I play golf? That question is often asked by non-golfers who cannot comprehend why a game has so many participants who love the sport to such a high degree. I feel these nonparticipants do not understand our devotion to a game called GOLF. Maybe these "reasons" will help you when that question is posed."

A Trip Into Tranquility: Everyone needs a change of scenery. Golf is played on Mother Nature's own turf. For a few brief hours you can change your environment and give your mind a chance to suppress and alleviate all forms of distress. It's better to allow the body's natural protective mechanism to work than to take man-made drugs.

A Change of Pace: It's a game that defies speed and a quickened pace. Four hours with friends all laughing at one another. If four hours is too long, you can always quit at the end of 9 holes and hurry back to the everyday stresses and worries that you were trying to get away from in the beginning.

Builds Character: That it does. You must accept adversity and success within minutes. Not only does the game build character, it also reveals it.

Sociability: One of the few games that allows you to visit and converse with friends as you play.

Even-Steven: The handicap system permits everyone to compete on an equal basis. The game embraces *everyone* and lets each player enjoy the competition.

Individualism: Hitting a golf ball does not require any special physique so *everyone is qualified!* "It ain't much...but it's all I got...I intend to make it work," philosophy. The hitting of a golf ball permits a variety of methods and the only thing that really matters in competition is how one scores.

Decision Making: The game allows each player to make his or her own decisions in a prompt manner. Each correct decision brings on a glow and feeling of satisfaction, and even on a bad day there are a lot of glows *if you look for them.*

It's Close: The golf course is relatively close compared to taking a trip to the beach or mountains to get away. Proximity is one of the games's greatest virtues.

Longevity: "A game of a lifetime." (My father has been a member of the PGA for half a century.) Each year more players are shooting their ages. I have a member who has been playing for 65 years and shot his age at 85, eleven times last year. What a thrill for everyone!

Exercise-Calories: Carrying your own bag and walking 18 holes will use up more calories than jogging 3 miles.

Competition: At every course there is friendly competition which can satisfy the competitive urge. There is no lack of competition if you have this type of interest and drive.

Sportsmanship: The game makes everyone face success and failure with each shot. You must also accept the good breaks with the bad. It gives you the opportunity to exhibit self-discipline in the face of adversity.

Entertainment: Golf is a game! Please don't lose sight of that fact. In this hectic world, we all need to play more games for enjoyment.

Be Yourself: It is one of the few sports you can play alone. You don't need a partner, and if you wish to spend a few hours by yourself, there could not be a better opportunity than a golf course or practice range.

Practice: Many players enjoy the challenge of the golf swing. An hour or two hitting practice balls and working on your technique is a wonderful remedy for tension and distress. There are some players who enjoy practicing even more than playing.

Integrity: One of the few sports that has no referees or umpires. You are on your own, as an honest man or woman. In this way the game allows you to like yourself a lot better if you play by the rules.

"I would like to state that I have seen this great game save a lot of lives from sadness, disaster and even death. All the reasons above will not apply on one given day, but every round of golf can touch lightly on many of them. The game is intoxicating to those who play and therefore, helps us renew and refresh our outlook towards this complicated world. The game is like a drug, but it's harmless and it's available for everyone to enjoy. It's not just a sport or a game, but a grand way of life."

An Emotion That Destroys

An unfortunate occurrence in golf is a player losing his temper. Getting angry because of what happens on a golf course, no matter what or who caused the anger, is plain nonsense if it destroys what is supposed to be an enjoyable experience. Negative actions by one golfer can spoil not only his own pleasure but also damage the fun for the rest of the group.

Dr. Orrin Hunt in his book, *The Joy of Golf,* suggests seven steps to eliminate temper from the personality while playing. He prefaces them with the following comments.

"What are the benefits of eliminating temper? I play better golf; my friends and family have rejoined me and, best of all, I feel *good* about myself. I truly do experience *Joy* when I play golf!"

"If you want to eliminate temper from your personality while playing golf (and, incidentally, enjoy the benefits of that absence that carries over into the rest of your life), do the following:

Step 1   Make a decision right now to commit yourself to the conviction that you are in charge of yourself.

Step 2   Subscribe to the concept that *you* and you alone own your feelings. Nothing outside of yourself can dictate to you how you feel, unless you give it or "them" permission to do so.

Step 3   Temper in all forms, including hostility, irritation, anger at yourself, and anger at others (persons, things, or circumstances), will be eliminated from your personality.

Step 4   On each round of golf you play from now on, mark a "T" on your personal score card at every hole where you become even slightly perturbed.

Step 5   Temporarily stop playing for scores. Your new game is to play for zero "T's" on your score card. If you have even one, you lose the round. If you have none, you win!

Step 6   Continue playing for a total absence of "T's" until you accomplish at least three "T"-free rounds. Then resume your usual score-conscious efforts.

Step 7   Never let a "T" occur on your score card again.

All you have to gain is the Joy of Golf in its *real* sense. All you have to lose is your temper."

Develop A Realistic Expectation Level

Golf is a simple game: knock a ball from here to there with a stick, and hole it out. Simple, yes; but not easy. It just looks easy, particularly on television when one watches the greatest players in the world hit incredible shots in routine fashion. When the show leaves the air, what happens? The golfing viewers flock to their courses immediately after switching off the set. They have spent two hours watching professionals who have practiced exhaustively since they were in grade school, who have had the finest teachers in the world, who play with the best equipment, who compete three out of every four weeks during the year, and who feel that par is a bad round. "All my life I wanted to play golf like Jack Nicklaus, and now I do," Paul Harvey (News commentator after Jack Nicklaus shot and 83 in the British Open). In comparison, the TV viewer is lucky to squeeze in two games a week, practices infrequently, takes too much of his instruction from friends, and uses clubs that are not matched to his swing. Yet this golfer somehow expects to perform like those players he saw on TV. How much more healthy and enjoyable it is to have a reasonable level of expectation. The over-competitive mind-set is unrealistic and puts too much pressure on what should be a *more relaxed* experience. "The person who enjoys his work as much as he does his hobby is a genius. The golfer who lets frustration destroy the pleasure of the game is a fool." No player is ever going to be perfect, so golfers should become familiar with the words of Tommy Armour who said, "Missing simple shots is part of being human." Golfers are going to err so they should be prepared for it.

Getting The Most From The Experience

Let's put things in perspective. The vast majority of golfers don't play for a living; they play for enjoyment. So the question is, "How are they going to get the most enjoyment from their golf?"

One approach is to encourage players not to put all their eggs in the basket of scoring. Sure, they want to play well, and when they do, they *will* enjoy it more. But if they only have fun when they are playing well, they are going to have fun about 10 percent of the time.

Have them look for other elements of the game from which they can derive satisfaction and pleasure other than a low number on a scorecard. Playing with people they enjoy is worth a lot; so is a beautiful day; a break from the routine; a walk among the trees; a bird, a flower, a butterfly, a beautiful setting; appreciating a good shot by an opponent; a laugh, a challenge, a long putt that drops, no matter that it's for a seven. Encourage players not to let the beautiful setting disappear because they've made a double bogey. We as people are not our golf games. How we react to our golf performance, however, may reflect **WHAT** *we really are.* In *Personal Par*, a book written by Barbara Keogh and Carol Smith, a psychological system to enjoy golf more is presented for women but could apply to anyone.

The Purpose Of It All

What is the purpose of golf? What is the value of this game to an individual—to the world? Is a vocation in golf worthy, or is it a waste of a lifetime? These questions have been seriously pondered by a number of golf professionals at sometime in their career. The answers will reveal how you perceive your occupation, your position within that occupation, and how well you perform in that position. But let's first look at the game itself.

"Golf is the only game having its etiquette modified in 12 articles of conduct representing several centuries of civilized experience."

The purpose of golf can be included within the answer, "In life, what is the purpose of play?" Human beings have a fundamental desire for play which is as old as man himself. Toys have been found among the ruins of ancient Babylonia, China and Egypt with evidence of various forms of games or contests to match. *Play is what people do for fun or enjoyment.* An adult enjoys it in his leisure away from work, a child as a part of life growing up. Golf is simply one of those play choices.

There are various forms of play:

1. Active motor play such as running, jumping, swimming and sports like golf.

2. Passive intellectual play such as cards, chess and crossword puzzles.

3. Sensory play, or being a spectator of a game or sport.

Not all people enjoy active motor play, therefore participation in sports does not appeal to them. This is something we must acknowledge...golf isn't for everyone. For others who generally do like sports, they might find golf not active enough, they prefer more rapid-moving or physically demanding games. But for millions of people around the world golf has a compelling attraction. A teacher of golf should help the student find the most appealing aspects of golf so as to make the student's investment of time productive, satisfying his need for fun and enjoyment. Some golfers seek the solitude of the game and don't wish to be forced into competition with others; some like the walk; others want "action"—competition to show who is the better performer; some may like golf because it gives them the chance to meet people and socialize; others just like to be outdoors in a beautiful setting. It's the blend of all of these benefits and more which is appealing. However, golfers find their joy, whatever it is that creates excitement at the prospect of play, *golf is their chosen game!*

If you, the teacher, can enhance what is intrinsically good about golf; if you present it in an interesting fashion, in a comfortable setting, at a level the pupil can easily comprehend, then you are filling a role of making life more enjoyable for those whom you serve. You are contributing in part toward what some have come to call "the good life." Golf has no exclusive on this condition. It can be found in other places through entirely different activities. But you, by being good at what you do, have met the challenge on your own turf.

Reproduced from the PGA Teaching Manual, with permission.

Appendix C

GOLF SWING MISCONCEPTIONS

by
Dr. Jim Suttie
PGA Professional
Formerly at Medinah Country Club
and
Golf Coach
Northwestern University
Currently, Director, The Learning Center,
Pine Needles
Southern Pines, NC

In previous articles, I emphasize that the golf swing is primarily a rotational movement of the body in which the big muscles of the shoulders and hips dominate. The small muscles of the hands and arms simply follow this movement and respond to this rotation. As a result, proper weight shift during the golf swing is attained by this body rotation.

In this article, we'll discuss some long held beliefs about the golf swing and try to explain how some of these beliefs have actually inhibited the learning of a correct golf swing motion. Let's get started:

Misconception #1: Keep the left arm (or lead arm) straight or stiff.

Reasons why this is not true: If the left (lead arm) is kept rigid and stiff throughout the entire swing motion, the arms will work independently of the body. Also, the stiffness in the arm will induce tension and limit the rotation of the left shoulder.

Misconception #2: Keep your head down.

Reasons: If the golfer has his head buried in his chest, he will inevitably lift it up as he comes into impact. The "head down" syndrome limits the ability of the shoulders to turn under the chin. Usually, this head position is a result of poor posture at set-up.

Misconception #3: Keep your head still.

Reasons: If the golfer keeps his head absolutely still, he will limit his ability to rotate and get his weight over the back leg. There are very few tour players who can keep their heads absolutely still. Most players allow their heads to move just slightly in order to get an acceptable shoulder turn. Usually the head moves with the upper spine on the backswing until it has moved about two inches from where it started.

Misconception #4: The center of your golf swing is the sternum or the center of your golf swing is the head.

Reasons: If we pivot around a point of our body (the sternum or the head), we will never be able to get the weight shifted over the right leg (for right-handed golfers). Actually, the center of the swing is the posterior lower spine just below the small of the lower back.

Misconception #5: There is lateral motion away from and towards the target during the swing.

Reasons: Since the golf swing is a circular motion with the club, we must create a rotary motion with our bodies. There is little, if any, lateral motion during the swing. Essentially, what appears to be lateral motion is simply rotation of the body until the right hip is over the right heel on the backswing and the left hip has rotated over the left heel on the forward swing (for right-handed golfers).

Misconception #6: The arms swing and the body simply responds to that motion or the hands and arms move first and then the shoulders and hips follow.
Reasons: If the hands and arms move first in the backswing, the shoulders will turn late in the backswing. As a result, the golfer will lose his extension and create an overly long and loose swing that is likely to come outside and over-the-top on the downswing.

Actually, the first part of the backswing should be a one-piece movement with the hands, arms, clubhead, shoulders and hips all moving away together. This insures a weight shift, arm and club extension and a firm and short swing.

Furthermore, if the swing produces centrifugal force, the center of the swing must move first to create the force. The true center of the swing is located in the posterior lower spine somewhere behind the hips. This part moves first and the hands, arms, and clubhead simply respond to this initial movement. The big muscles of the shoulders, back and hips are the slowest moving, yet most powerful muscles in the body. These muscles move first and keep the faster moving muscles of the hands and arms under control. Correct movement is always produced from the center of the body outward—never from the clubhead inward.

Misconception #7: Feel like you are sitting on a bar stool with the weight back on the heels at the start of the swing.

Reasons: If we sit back on the heels at address, we are likely to have the knees over-flexed. With weight on the heels and over-flexed knees, we are not able to rotate the lower body because of abducted hips. Also, when starting with weight on the heels, there's usually no place to move except to the toes.

Misconception #8: The ball position changes for the different clubs in the bag. For example, the ball should be positioned forward for the driver and back towards the center of the stance for the nine iron.

What appears to be a change in ball position with the shorter clubs is really only a narrower, more open stance with the weight distributed more on the front leg at the start of the swing. The ball actually looks like it is being played in the center of the stance for a nine iron and off the left heel for the driver. In reality, the ball position will be approximately the same for both the woods and the irons. It is the open and narrow stance that makes the ball appear back in the stance with the short irons. Essentially, there is only one bottom to your swing arc if we are going to create any consistently struck golf shots.

Misconception #9: The club moves straight away from the ball on the takeaway.

Reasons: The golf swing is a side of the line hitting game. By this, I mean that we are standing to the side of the ball. Because of the way we are set up, we must arc the club inside the target line as we take it back. In addition to this, the hands and the arms follow the body rotation both on the backswing and the downswing. If we follow the principle, then the turning of the shoulders and hips will naturally cause the club to come a little inside the target line on the backswing.

Misconception #10: The weight starts on the right leg (for right-handed golfers) at the start of the swing.

Reasons: If the weight started on the back leg at the address, it would be impossible to make a rotational move with the body. Because of this, the golfer would become a hand and arm player. Also, if the weight is set to the right at address, it is likely to move to the left on the backswing. This is the reverse weight shift that most golfers have in their golf swings.

Actually, the weight shift should start slightly forward on the front leg. From this position, the golfer has somewhere to move—to the right side.

Misconception #11: Restrict your hips on the backswing and coil your shoulders against them.

Reasons: If the golfer restricts his hip turn on the backswing, he will limit the range of motion of the shoulder turn. Only the very flexible and coordinated golfer is able to do this.

In reality, the hips control the shoulders both on the backswing and downswing. Therefore, if the golfer restricts his hip turn, he will restrict his shoulder turn. With a restricted shoulder turn, the golfer is likely to start the downswing with the shoulders unwinding ahead of the hips. This will produce pulls and pull slices.

Misconception #12: We should return to the address position at impact.

Reasons: At impact, we see pictures of the tour stars that show them with the majority of their weight on their lead leg with hips opened to the target line and shoulders parallel to the target line. In fact, the hips are just slightly forward of the position they started in. The mistake most people make here is they slide their hips too far forward on the downswing creating weight shift and balance problems at impact.

In reality, the shoulders out-turn the hips on the backswing. This allows the hips to move first on the downswing and to open up and stay ahead of the shoulders at impact.

Misconception #13: The golfer should consciously try to release the club. This definition of release means to pronate and supinate the hands and arms and to consciously try to turn the club over through the impact area.

Reasons: Correct body (shoulder and hip) rotation will automatically create correct hand and arm rotation. Any conscious effort to open or close the clubface, either on backswing or downswing, will most likely create an inconsistency in your ball striking. Any conscious effort to try to release the clubhead is a compensation for poor body rotation.

If the golf swing is a circular motion in which centrifugal force is produced, the inertia and the weight of the swing clubhead will automatically create the release.

Misconception #14: The power source in the golf swing comes from the hands, arms, and wrists. We should try to snap our wrists as we come into the impact area.

Reasons: Power in the golf swing comes from leverage (swing arc), torsion (body rotation), and weight shift. In order to achieve these three goals, we must rotate our bodies. The real power source in the golf swing is the hips. The faster we move the hips in the downswing, the faster the hands and arms will work. There is no conscious use of the wrists and hands through the impact area. The hands and arms rotate in response to body rotation.

Misconception #15: The golfer should stay behind the ball long after the ball is hit. A corollary to this is that the golfer should keep his head down and right (or left) shoulder back for as long as possible after impact.

Reasons: It is true that the head is behind the ball at the point of contact. But, just after impact, the forceful unwinding of the shoulders should allow the head to rotate with the shoulders and come up out of the shot. Any effort to keep the head and right shoulder back behind the ball after the point of contact will cause the weight to stay on the back leg. This error will cause all kinds of poor shots including pulls, pull hooks and push fades.

In reality, the shoulders turn about 200 degrees on the forward swing. The shoulders actually catch up to and pass the hips just after impact. At the finish of the swing, the right shoulder should be just slightly higher than the left with the chest facing to the left of the target line and the hips facing directly down the target line. This finish position insures that the shoulders have out-turned the hips and a correct weight shift to the left leg has been made.

Misconception #16: The golfer should pull the club down from the top of the swing with the left (or right) hand and arms. Another related statement would ask the golfer to pull the butt of the club at the ball on the downswing.

Reasons: If the golfer pulls the butt of the club down on the downswing or pulls down with the left (or right) hand or arm on the downswing, he creates angles with his arms. In this case, pulling down with the left hand and arm will force the left elbow up to the sky which will leave the clubface open through impact. Better advice might be "start the downswing with the lower body and try to keep the elbows down throughout the entire swing motion." If the golfer turns his hips through the ball instead of sliding through it, the clubface will naturally close and the left arm will fold downward after impact.

In addition to this, the golf swing is a bilateral motion and shouldn't be dominated by either the right or left side of the body.

Misconception #17: The path of the clubhead on a correct golf swing is inside-outside.

Reasons: Most of us have been taught to swing inside-outside. Unfortunately, this is not correct. If the golfer swings excessively inside-outside, he will push fade and hook most of his golf shots. It might feel like we are swing inside-outside, but what really should happen is this: The golf club approaches the ball from inside the target line through impact, and then moves off to the left of the target line after impact. This occurs because the hands and arms follow the body rotation both on the backswing and downswing. It is this "inward-to straight-to inward" club movement that creates a natural release of the clubhead through impact and divots that point slightly left on the target line.

Misconception #18: The weight stays centered throughout the entire swinging motion.

Reasons: If the weight stayed centered throughout the entire swing, the golfer would be unable to make a weight shift. Also, the golf swing is an elliptical arc (egg-shaped). This type of arc is created because the golfer is working out of two shoulder sockets and two hip sockets. On the backswing, the shoulder and hip turn create a weight shift over the right heel. Finally, on the downswing, the movement of the feet, knees and hips create a weight shift over the left heel.

Misconception #19: The golfer should try to shift his weight.

Reason: The weight shift is created by shoulder and hip rotation. The shoulders turn and the one-piece takeaway is responsible for most of the weight shift on the backswing while the hip turn is responsible for the weight shift on the downswing. There is a minimal amount, if any, of sliding the hips during the swing.

Misconception #20: The club is swung on a single swingplane.

Reason: First of all, everybody has their own unique swingplane because of posture, body build, how far they stand away from the ball, and their timing system. But, generally speaking, the downswing plane does come below the backswing plane because the weight is moving to the left pivot point. This movement to the left side abducts the arms (arms get closer) to the body and drops the plane below the way it went back. But each case is very individual as there have been many successful golfers who have come down outside the way they went back. The important thing to remember is that it is impossible to swing on a single plane on both the backswing and downswing. Also, about 24 inches prior to impact, the clubhead is approaching the ball from inside the target line.

*These articles reprinted courtesy of Chicago Metro Golfer and PGA Teaching Manual

Appendix D

Author Documentation

KIWANIS CLUB OF COLUMBIA

P.O. BOX 158   **COLUMBIA, MISSOURI 65205**

TO: Whom It May Concern

FROM: Rex Dillow, Chairman, Golf Committee.

This memorandum is to certify that W. R. "Wil" Miller played in 8 matches in the Kiwanis Division V (Mid-Missouri) round-robin competition during the summers of 1989 and 1990. Wil's average score played on six different courses was 77.6.*
In Missouri State Kiwanis Tournaments, Wil was the winner in 1989 with a score of 75, and in 1990 with a score of 76.

Rex Dillow
December 13, 1990

*Kiwanis competition allows the ball to be picked and placed.

TO: Whom It May Concern

FROM: Rex Dillow, Secretary-Treasurer

This memorandum is to certify that W. R. "Wil" Miller had a season ending handicap* of 2 for 1989 and 3 for 1990. The handicaps were established on the A. L. Gustin course at the University of Missouri-Columbia with a rating of 68.5. Wil posted a score of 75 in the season ending league tournament in 1990.

Rex Dillow
December 13, 1990

*   League rules allow the ball to be picked and placed.